Colorado

AN AERIAL GEOGRAPHY OF THE HIGHEST STATE

Tom Huber and Jim Wark

WESTERN REFLECTIONS
PUBLISHING COMPANY

"Geography is a point of view, a way of looking at things. If one focuses on how all kinds of things exist together spatially, in areas, with a special emphasis on context and coherence, one is working as a geographer. ... The born-geographer lives geography every day. It is the way one makes sense out of one's world, near and far, and it is the means of appreciating the immediate world - of whatever lies before one's eyes."

Donald Meinig
From: A Life of Learning (1972)

First Edition

Library of Congress Catalog Number: 2001097740

ISBN 1- 890437-59-X

Cover & Book Design by SJS Design (Susan Smilanic)
Printed in China

Western Reflections Publishing Company
P.O. Box 1647
Montrose, CO 81402-1647
www.westernreflectionspub.com

Table of Contents

Crestone Peak 14,294' and South Colony Lakes, Sangre de Cristo Range, Custer County. This view looks northwest into the San Luis Valley

Winter morning alpenglow over snow-blanketed Sawatch Range, Chaffee County.

eography is the study of place in all of its guises. We, the authors, are lucky enough to live and work in one of the most physically beautiful places in America - Colorado (Photo 3). But Colorado is not just a series of picture postcards or calendar art pages; it is a complex, interesting, rapidly changing, and intriguing place where intricate physical and human landscapes interweave and interact. Our purpose with this book is to look at this interwoven tapestry of Colorado, and through photographs and text, articulate a different look at the geography of the place we love.

Most people most of the time experience a place from what geographers call the profile view. We look at scenes from the side, or maybe the inside, of the landscape. Our vision is often blocked by the various individual elements in the scene – we cannot see the town for the houses, the mountain for the rocks, or even the forest for the trees. To get the whole view of most landscapes, we must move about to capture a piece of the picture at a time. In spite of the fact that we cannot see the total at any one time, we are used to looking at scenes this way, and it makes sense to us visually. The only problem, then, is being able to see the bigger, more holistic picture.

Geographers, whose job it is to study the whole of a place, often solve this problem by using maps or map-like pictures and images of landscapes. These are usually drawn or portrayed directly from above. This vertical viewing angle is such that the entire landscape can be seen at one time. Once one learns how to "see" from this perspective, informative spatial patterns are revealed. Everything from road and transportation networks to drainage patterns, and from the mix of crops in a farming area to the lie of the land in a mountainous terrain can be seen and studied more precisely. This view is very useful, but it is also unfamiliar to most people. It gives us more information in one context but takes away information from a more common way of seeing.

The photographs in this book are all taken from the air but at an angle to give us the best of both of the other viewing perspectives. Photographers and geographers call these oblique aerial photographs. We get the benefits of almost normal profile viewing with those of vertical aerial photographs seen directly from above. Not only are these hybrid views beautiful, they tell the complex stories of the landscapes in a way no other view can (Photo 8). We not only want you to see the gorgeous sights of this gorgeous state; we want you to see the patterns, the connectedness, and the interactions of the lands and the peoples of Colorado. This series of photographs and the accompanying text will give you this extraordinary way of understanding.

COLORADO - A PRIMER

Although prior to 1861 the place of Colorado was almost exclusively occupied by numerous Native American tribes and clans, it was claimed by no fewer than ten different countries or states as part of their land. These claims ranged from Spain's in the 16th century, New England's in the 17th century, and France's in the 18th century to various claims by Missouri, Texas, Utah, Kansas, and New Mexico thereafter. By February of 1861, however, all of these claims had been put aside and Colorado became its own territory within the United States. It subsequently became part of the Union as a state in 1876 - hence the nickname "Centennial State." But Colorado's true identity has always been plagued by its

COLORADO - THE HIGHEST STATE

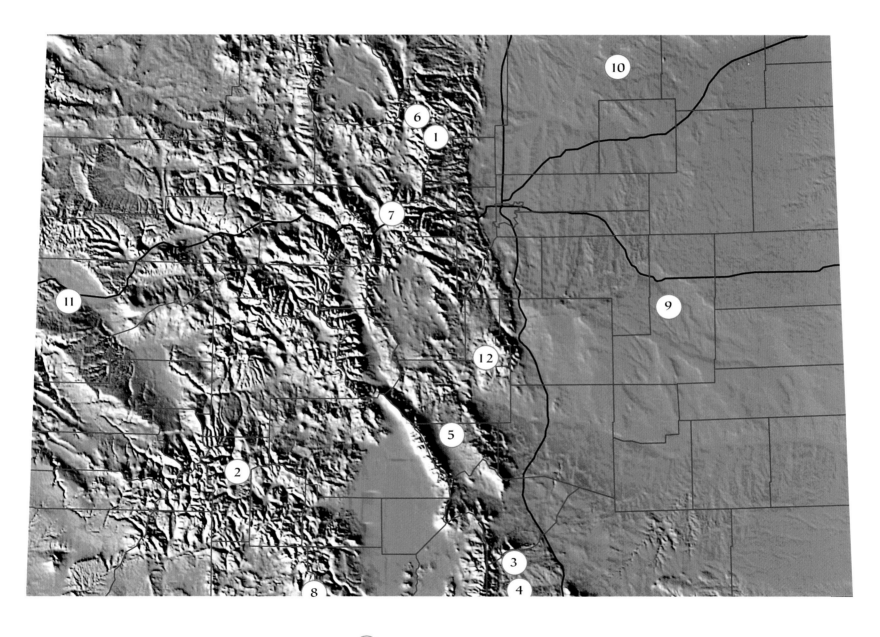

photo position

seemingly arbitrarily assigned borders. Paradoxically, it is one of the most complex topographic, climatic, and biotic states (Photo 2). Yet it is defined by the most simplistic of borders - two north-south meridians and two east-west parallels with no divergence for natural variation. In no way do the two latitudinal parallels and the two meridians define or rationally contain what this state is. Nonetheless, these unsophisticated boundaries are the ones with which we must deal.

Overly naïve descriptions are also often used when dealing with the extreme complexity of the state's natural phenomena. For example, even though a climate is an average of how the weather acts over time, there are numerous localized climates in and around Colorado. And the climates of the state not only include the complicated and enigmatic highland areas but also the plains, the plateaus, and all of the variants deriving from changes in latitude and elevation. We have deserts and near-deserts in places such as the San Luis Valley and the Colorado Plateau. We have semi-arid conditions in the eastern plains. And everywhere in Colorado we get the general increases in precipitation and decreases in temperature associated with ascending ever-higher elevations. Within the average values that create the climates and the artificial borders that create the state there is only one constant - variability.

The multi-year averages of climate are derived from the daily, maybe even hourly, weather patterns that rush across Colorado in seemingly endless variation. To put it succinctly, the weather of Colorado is in constant flux. A place that gets 15 inches of precipitation on average for the year (a climatic variable) might receive 15 inches of rain in a single thunderstorm on a summer afternoon (a weather or meteorological variable). The average high temperature in mid-June might be around 85° for eastern Colorado, but it might only reach 60° for days on end in any given year. We may get virtually no snow for an entire winter along the Front Range and then get two feet in a day in May (Photo 5). The defined climates for the state of Colorado give us only a gross idea of what we can expect at any one time. The weather patterns we deal with on a regular basis are some of what keeps Colorado an interesting place to live.

Of course the people who live in and visit Colorado are not the only species who are affected by the climate/weather here. The native flora and fauna and those species that have migrated here all depend on the delicate balance and timing of heat, light, precipitation, and wind that come from the weather patterns crossing the state. Each species of plant has its own requirements, and often a collection of species will develop under similar circumstances. This collection of plant species and the animals which depend on it is referred to as a community. A community occurs at a given spot and usually has a dominant physical characteristic. In Colorado we have hundreds of different community types. A broader, more inclusive term for looking at a collection of interrelated plants and animals is the ecosystem. An ecosystem refers to the total physical character of related plants and animals over a larger area than a community. It is almost always a collection of communities and is usually described by its dominant vegetation type. In Colorado, for example, we have the ponderosa pine ecosystem, the spruce-fir ecosystem (Photo 6), the plains-riparian ecosystem (Photo 9), and the piñon-juniper ecosystem. There are a few dozen ecosystems in Colorado. Both communities and ecosystems are complicated arrangements of dependency and mutual reliance whereby plants and animals rely on and affect other plant and animal species. The intricacies of each of these are beyond what we can discuss in a book of this size and type. Thousands of scientific articles and monographs exist to describe and study the numerous communities and ecosystems of Colorado.

Throughout the book, we will discuss a few of the more important ecosystems of the state, but we will use a much broader brush to organize our efforts. This brush is called the life zone. The concept of the life zone is an old one. The peoples of the Andes Mountains of South America may have been the first to use it. Alexander von Humboldt described the nomenclature used by the mountain dwellers of the Andes in his work in the mid-19th century. Terms such as *tierra caliente* (the hot land at low elevations), *tierra templada* (the temperate land at mid-elevations), and *tierra fria* (the cold lands at high elevations) are three life zones used by the Andean Indians to describe their homeland. Others have refined the concept and defined life zones for other places. John Marr (1961) did this for the East Slope of Colorado. Although the life zone concept is a gross way to look at the intricacies of any land, it is a useful framework for understanding the big picture of Colorado. We will use a slightly modified version of Marr's classification as the organization for this book. Each of the subsequent six chapters of the book is a different life zone in Colorado and is based on general elevation categories with one exception - the Sonoran life zone of Chapter 7. Because life zones must encompass so many places with varying ecosystems and climate/weather patterns, the elevation ranges for adjacent zones will often overlap. These transitional areas between the life zones are called ecotones by ecologists (Photo 7). Some of the ecotones are just as interesting as the life zones themselves and will be discussed where appropriate.

The lowest elevation zone is the plains life zone (from 3,350 feet to about 6,000 feet). The plains life zone is covered in Chapter 2 and is mostly composed of the vast grasslands associated with the Great Plains. The climate is semi-arid with drought conditions occurring too frequently for the comfort of most farmers and ranchers. The next highest zone is the foothills life zone (from about 5,500 feet to nearly 8,000 feet). This is the often dramatic transition zone between plains and mountains discussed in Chapter 3. Most of the people of Colorado are familiar with this zone because it is the backdrop for the major cities along the Front Range. As we ascend past the foothills, we enter the montane life zone (from about 7,500 to almost 9,500 feet). Chapter 4 of the book covers this zone which is the place where the real mountains of Colorado begin. Most of the small mountain communities sit in the montane, and many of our visions of what mountains are like come from this zone. Skiers in the state are very familiar with the next zone covered in Chapter 5, the subalpine life zone (9,500 to about 12,000 feet). Most of the major ski areas in the state are in the subalpine because that is where most of the deep, consistent snowfalls are. In Chapter 6 we enter the highest places in Colorado, the regions of the state above the trees - the alpine life zone (from 11,500 feet to 14,433 feet at the top of Mt. Elbert). These seemingly barren, yet spectacular, lands are the stunning landscapes so many envision when they think of our high mountains. Lastly, we have the upper Sonoran life zone (between 6,000 and 7,500 feet) so named because it somewhat resembles the higher reaches of the Sonoran Desert of Arizona and California. This is the land of the Colorado Plateau of western Colorado and much of Utah with its climate of desert or near-desert conditions.

The climate-vegetation categories are not the only physical characteristics that need to be put into our discussion. The geology and geomorphology (landforms) of the regions throughout Colorado also need to be looked at as part of the total natural environment. As with the climate and vegetation distributions around Colorado, the geologic setting of the state is complex. In fact if one were to look at a geologic map of the entire United States, there are few places in the country that have more complicated geology. So again we must simplify. There are five basic geologic provinces in Colorado, and only three of these affect large areas of the state.

The most easterly, of course, is the Great Plains geologic province. This province underlies much of the plains life zone and is composed almost exclusively of nearly flat-lying sedimentary rock formations (Photo 10). The sediments that make up many of these rocks come from times in our far past when the area was at a much lower elevation — this even includes some times when parts of the state were below sea level. Other sedimentary rock formations of the province were formed during the periodic mountain uplifts that have occurred over the last 1.7 billion years. As these mountains went up, erosion began to wear them down. The detritus from this uplift/erosion cycle created at least two of the major formations visible along the Front Range

mountain front - the Fountain and the Dawson formations.

The most westerly of the three main geologic provinces in Colorado is the Colorado Plateau (Photo 11). This province, too, is composed of sedimentary rocks derived from similar processes to those in the Great Plains province. The main difference for the Colorado Plateau is the extensive nature of the uplifted plateau which not only includes western Colorado and much of Utah, but also parts of New Mexico and Arizona as well. The plateau was lifted by massive, regional forces that were sub-continental in scope. Coincidentally, much of the plateau is covered with the Sonoran life zone described above.

Between these two relatively flat regions lies the third major geologic province - the Southern Rocky Mountains. The mountains of Colorado have had a long and torturous history of uplift and erosion cycles. The mountains we see today are at least the fifth version of Rocky Mountains since the mid-Precambrian era. The dominant rock type of our mountains is igneous intrusive rock, mostly granite and granite-like rock. The Gore, Park, Sawatch, and Front Ranges (Photo 1) are examples. But there are ample instances of sedimentary rock mountains such as the Maroon Bells and portions of the Sangre de Cristos for example. The more recent mountains, on the order of 25 to 30 million years old, are the volcanic mountains, with the San Juans and West Elks being the most extensive. Competing forces of regional uplift, volcanic activity, sedimentary deposition, glacial advances, and running water all have combined to create the complex jumble of landscapes in the mountains of Colorado. Many of the photographs in this book will give visual proof of the beauty and magnificence that these intertwining forces have wrought.

Art historians use the term "palimpsest" to describe a picture painted over an already existing picture. This was often done to save the price of a new canvas. Obviously, the geology of Colorado has continually changed over time. The climates, vegetation, and animals have also changed with the passing eons, and what we see now lies on the detritus

of many past worlds much like a series of paintings on an old canvas. The same can be said of human occupation. People have lived in Colorado for at least 11,000 years. Ancient Clovis and Folsom peoples left behind their distinctive projectile points as proof of their existence. Later generations of native peoples have bequeathed to us magnificent physical examples of their culture. Some, like the cliff dwellings of the Ancestral Puebloans or Anasazi of southwestern Colorado, continue to be central to the study of ancient cultures in the state. European influences began in the 16th century and have only grown since then. Today we see an ever more urbanized state where the cities and suburbs are the dominant cultural artifact. In each chapter of the book, we will include the important impacts that human occupation has brought to the landscapes of the state. The combination of natural and human influences are a strongly mixed patina on this palimpsest we know as Colorado. (Photos 4 and 12).

PHOTO 1 Longs Peak in Rocky Mountain National Park is one of several massive monoliths along the Front Range of Colorado. Mount Evans, Mount Bierstadt, and Pikes Peak are among the other "14ers" that punctuate the eastern-most range of the Southern Rocky Mountains.

PHOTO 2 The Rio Grande headwaters in the eastern San Juan Mountains is an area of incredible complexity. The high, rocky alpine zone hovers over treed and meadowed lands. The waters from the infant river and its tributaries feed the riparian vegetation providing a green vibrancy to the scene.

PHOTO 3 Some of the dramatic beauty of Colorado is easily seen in this photo of East Spanish Peak in the early autumn. A hint of the fall color is showing just below the peak. The higher and even more dramatic Sangre de Cristo Mountain Range is just visible in the background. The forested slopes surrounding the mountain lend an air of the natural bucolic.

PHOTO 4 The Stonewall area on the "back" side of the Spanish Peaks is an intense and beautiful example of the human/nature mix of landscape elements. The natural, especially in the form of the upturned sedimentary rocks, dominates and dictates how and where humans will live, work, and travel.

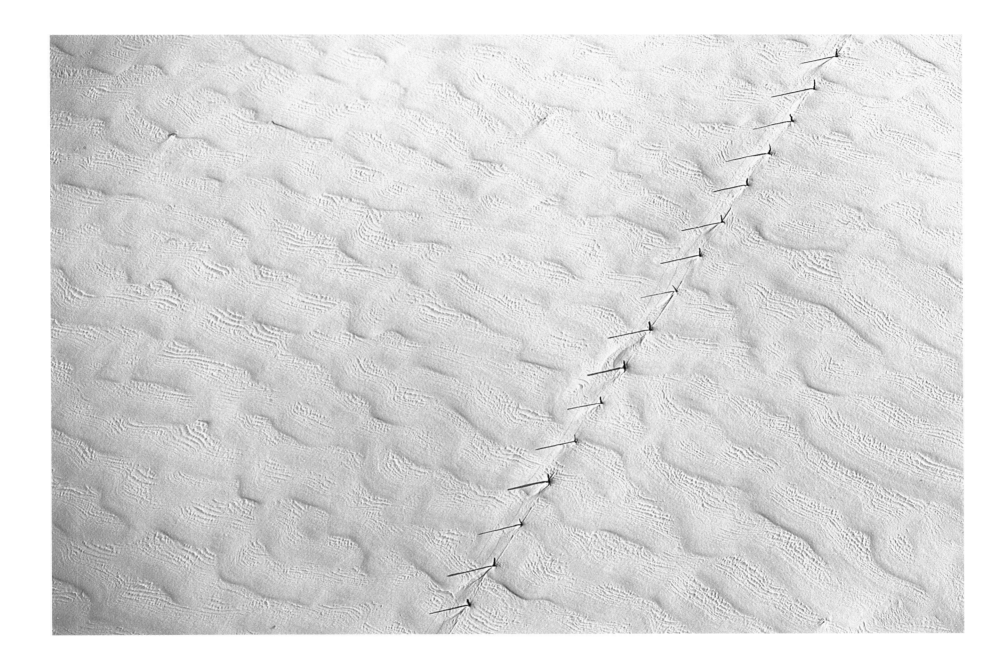

PHOTO 5 Snow usually comes in large doses when it comes. This stark landscape in the Wet Mountain Valley is only disturbed by the seemingly irrelevant fence posts.

PHOTO 6 The tall, slender spruces and firs of the high mountains here in Rocky Mountain National Park are highlighted by the bare rock that was carved and smoothed by glaciers in the not-too-distant past.

PHOTO 7 The inter-fingering of the forest with the alpine just above the Eisenhower Tunnel's east portal along Interstate 70 is an excellent example of the transition zone, or ecotone, in the mountains of the state.

PHOTO 8 Cumbres Pass is one of the least traveled in the state. Leading south from the San Luis Valley and the San Juan Mountains, it has been a historic and pre-historic route to and from places in what is now called New Mexico. Evidence of human habitation intermixes with the textures of natural landscapes.

PHOTO 9 Riparian areas in all of the life zones of Colorado are critical habitat for a myriad of fauna. They carry the most diverse species and the highest numbers too. Even this almost ethereal riparian ribbon in Lincoln County is crucial to the survival of Colorado's natural legacy.

PHOTO 10 The nearly horizontal sedimentary rock beds of the Pawnee National Grassland region are dramatic examples of the type of rock below most of the eastern plains of Colorado. Water erosion is responsible for the complex pattern of bare rock mingled with prairie grasslands.

PHOTO 11 The Colorado National Monument is on the far northeastern edge of the vast Colorado Plateau. This view shows the nature of the plateau - nearly horizontal sedimentary rock incised by innumerable canyons. The effect is often stunning.

PHOTO 12   The story of what Colorado is today could not be told truthfully without telling of the importance of mining in our history. Near duplicates of these abandoned gold mining works near Victor are repeated and repeated throughout the mineral zones of our mountains. The human and natural interaction at mining sites is one of the most important stories we have to tell in Colorado.

Center pivot irrigation circles dominate the landscape of the San Luis Valley north of Alamosa. Each circle is 1/4 mile in diameter with a water well at the center feeding a rotating sprinkler arm. The principal product in this scene is potatoes.

Chapter 2

PLAINS

BIG SKIES,

BIG LAND

(3,350 FEET

TO

6,000 FEET)

*I*f you had been among those intrepid travelers with the first wagon trains to come across the high plains of Colorado, you might well have thought, "this land is endless!!" Moving at ten or twelve miles a day, it took months to cross the Great Plains of Nebraska, Kansas, and Colorado. That trek was at various times lonely, long, boring, or dangerous. The dangers came from the weather (heat or cold, drought or deluge), sickness, and a few isolated instances of bad encounters with other humans. The trip may have been boring because your sights would have been focused on the land just before you; you would not have had the grander view of this enigmatic place. Given the right perspective, the plains of Colorado are anything but dull and monotonous. Aerial views of broad expanses of the land show a variety of landforms and landscapes (Photo 13). Scenes of endless grasslands or grain fields waving in the wind, expansive ranches with long vistas of the sky, riparian habitats for numerous flora and fauna, and ever changing skies of eye-stinging blues or dark and foreboding thunderheads are all

parts of this land. Some parts are just plainly spectacular. The deep canyons and varied scenes of the Purgatoire River Canyon in southeastern Colorado, for example, are some of the most visually pleasing of all of Colorado's landscapes (Photo 23).

This is not to imply that the plains have the wide-spread charisma of the high mountains of western Colorado, but it is always a good idea to really look closely at a place before making judgments about its character. To underestimate the natural and human landscapes of the plains diminishes the wonder of the entire mosaic of the state that is Colorado.

CLIMATE

Many people have described the dwindling precipitation rates on the Great Plains as one moves from east to west. One of the first to articulate this phenomenon in writing was Major Stephen Long in his report of his 1820 expedition. He coined the term "the Great American Desert" for the land west of the Hundreth Meridian. Wallace Stegner wrote a book using that artificial human marker as a "line in the sand" to demarcate the lands that need little or no irrigation from those that require it for agriculture. His book, *Beyond the Hundredth*

Meridian, is a classic about western political/economic/environmental interaction. All of this attention to the precipitation rates of the plains in general and the high plains of Colorado in particular is well justified. Climate, especially precipitation pattern, is probably the most important natural characteristic of this land. The amount, and distribution of water available for plants and animals define this as a place.

Average precipitation rates in eastern Colorado are pretty uniform. Almost all recording stations report averages of 15 to 16 inches annually. These statistics are very deceiving, however, because the variability of individual rain or snow events and yearly totals is profound. A single, although very rare, thunderstorm may deluge an area with 15 inches of rain, or no rain may fall in the same location for months. The only constant is inconsistency! Along with the inconsistent precipitation, eastern Colorado also has high winds, blizzard conditions in winter, intense solar radiation and heat in summer, and many, many beautiful days throughout the year.

PLAINS ECOSYSTEMS

The variability of the weather in eastern Colorado makes for

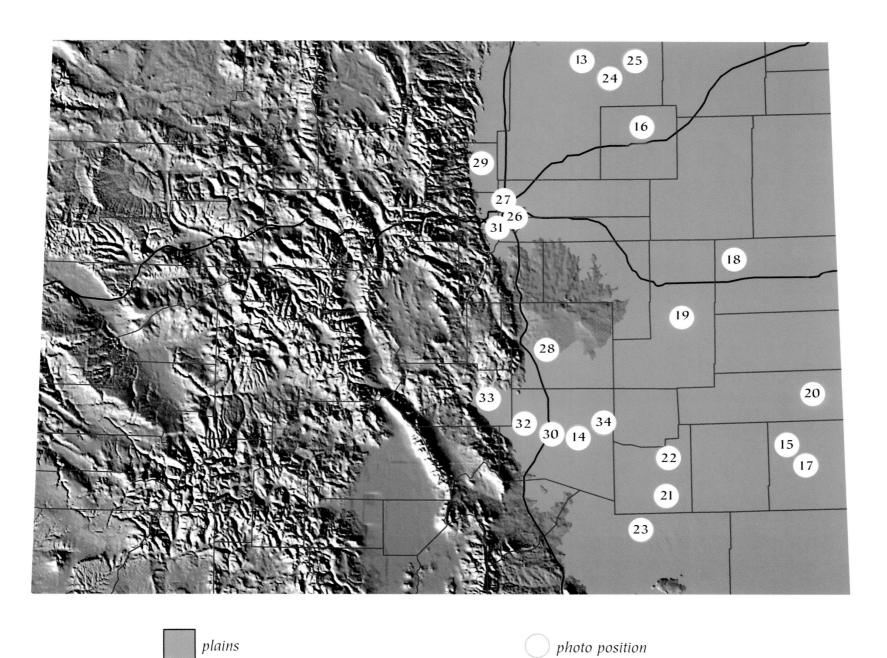

plains

photo position

some very difficult conditions for plants and animals. In essence, because sufficient and dependable moisture are not a given, plants must adapt to the lowest common denominator of conditions. This is the main reason that most of the plains are (or at least were) grasslands. Grasses can tolerate drought better than most other vegetation (Photo 14). They have extensive root systems that go deep into the soil for water and can store needed reserves of food and nutrients for the long, dry spells.

During the good moisture years, the plains flourish with a beautiful green wave of grasses and wildflowers. These are the conditions that lured homesteaders here in the late 1800s and early 1900s. "Dry" land farming techniques produced good crop yields and promising lives. But the natural variation of the plains' weather eventually caught up with these pioneers, and droughts devastated many families and communities (Photo 21). Extended drought during the 1890s and even longer, drier periods in the 1930s, forced thousands of farms to be abandoned and turned the hopes of the people into dust.

The devastation of the Dust Bowl was nearly total for both the people and the grass-stripped land. The pioneers drifted away and found new, if not better, lives. The land remained. The Federal Government's Soil Erosion Service, which became the Soil Conservation Service, which is now the Natural Resources Conservation Service, worked hard during these bad times to revive the land from its tortured state. Two large tracts of prairie were especially central to these efforts in Colorado. The Comanche National Grassland in southeastern Colorado and the Pawnee National Grassland in northeastern Colorado were large-scale experiments at putting the land back into grasses or at least farming the land using better, less destructive techniques. The results of these complex management efforts have created prairies that somewhat replicate what had been lost (Photo 25). Both the Comanche and the Pawnee Grasslands are testaments to what good land stewardship can accomplish (Photo 24).

Climate is a main reason why the plains are mostly grasslands, but it is certainly not the only one. Another critical component in developing large expanses of grasslands throughout the world is fire. Most natural grasslands can survive, even thrive intermittent fire that destroys woody vegetation such as trees or shrubs. The same root system of the grasses that helps them to survive drought are below ground and are protected from fires that burn the above ground stems and leaves. The roots are even stimulated after a fire to grow new and robust plants that out-compete other vegetation forms - fire is not only tolerated by grasses but is needed for vibrant grasslands.

Fires have occurred on grasslands throughout time - many have been caused by lightening, others caused unintentionally or intentionally by humans (Photo 15). Native Americans are often viewed as non-intrusive users of the land. More evidence is now being discovered that says they had major impacts on the land including using fire extensively as a tool for hunting. All around the world grasslands are deemed "pyrogenetic" landscapes by ecologists because, without fire, these landscapes would eventually disappear as we know them. They might even be invaded and dominated by advancing trees and forestlands.

The short grass prairie is not the only ecosystem of the plains. One of the most important, yet small in area, ecosystems in eastern Colorado is the riparian that follows the few perennial and many ephemeral watercourses of this land (Photo 16). The collected water, either above or below ground, in these streams provides the moisture for a variety of vegetation including cottonwoods, willows, alders, and water loving plants such as cattails and bulrushes. The riparian provides food and shelter for a varied and prolific wildlife collection. Deer, foxes, numerous birds, frogs, turtles, mink, skunks, and a multitude of others occupy these narrow strips in the environment. The riparian ribbons tend to go east-west and thus also provide transportation corridors that would not exist without the relative verdancy and safety of this ecosystem. One example of this water-caused highway system is the movement of the white-tailed deer that is an eastern species that has migrated west along these water courses. They

now inhabit riparian areas all the way to the mountain front and are in competition with the local mule deer.

The prairies were once home to other large mammals that have all but disappeared from the plains under pressure from humans. Elk were once plentiful on the plains and used the riparian areas for shelter while grazing the grasslands. Grizzly bear were a common and frightening sight for explorers and early settlers. Elk are now confined to the mountains and grizzly bear probably no longer exist in Colorado. The dominant faunal symbol for the prairie, however, is the bison or buffalo as we normally call it. Millions of buffalo migrated over the prairies in huge, constantly moving herds. These herds were not only the dietary mainstay for the scattered Native American tribes of the plains, they were also an important symbiotic part of the grassland ecosystem. Much evidence has now been collected to show that the eating habits and the soil loosening of millions of bison hooves helped keep the grasslands healthy and stable. Buffalo and prairie go together in myth and fact.

HUMAN PRESENCE

Although climates constantly, if slowly, change over time, the prairies of Colorado have been more or less semi-arid throughout the history of human occupation. This means that agriculture without supplemental irrigation is a very iffy matter. The original human occupants had no need for irrigation because they were nomadic hunters and gatherers. Our modern view of the 17th, 18th, and 19th century plains Indians is one of exquisite hunters on horseback riding intrepidly into huge buffalo herds for the kill. This view is relatively accurate as far as it goes, but before the Spanish introduced the horse as a domestic animal to the "New World" in the 16th century, the plains Indians were foot-bound. Before the horse, hunting was still the dominant economy for these peoples. They used many ingenious methods to kill the large numbers of animals needed to sustain whole villages. One of the most efficient was using fire or noise to drive herds of deer, antelope, or buffalo to their deaths over small cliffs that are scattered throughout the plains. Many of these killing and butchering sites can still be found in eastern Colorado.

The short grass prairie of Colorado's plains has had, if not lush forage, at least expansive grasslands capable of sustaining large herds of herbivores. Most of the grass species on the prairie are high in nutrients and provide good grazing for these herds. With the exception of observers such as Major Long and many of the early pioneers, most "Anglos" coming to the high plains recognized the vast resources available for raising livestock. It was inevitable that the Native American communal lands of the prairie would be coveted by Anglo ranchers and sheepherders. The "Indian Wars," as they are often termed, partially arose from these circumstances. Other factors that contributed to the conflicts were the general westward expansionist pressures from densely populated Eastern states, the belief in Manifest Destiny, and gold fever. Whatever the specific causes, the conflicts turned bloody and brutal on both sides. One of the most lingering and painful events of this entire era was the Sand Creek Massacre that occurred on November 29, 1864. This was a retaliatory strike for Indian raids committed earlier that year, probably by a completely different tribe. A large encampment of Cheyenne, supposedly under federal protection, was lodged along Sand Creek in what is now Kiowa County (Photo 20). The number of Cheyenne men, women, and children killed is still widely debated but the total was probably over two hundred. The ultimate result of such incidents was that by 1869, through treaty and conflict, the Cheyenne and Arapaho peoples of the plains of Colorado had all been removed. The way was open for Anglo settlement.

With the exception of a few gold camps, such as Auraria and Denver, established on the plains, most of the initial settlement of eastern Colorado was by cattlemen and sheepherders. One of the first and most influential was the Charles Goodnight-Oliver Loving Company which brought huge cattle herds to Colorado starting in 1866. Their operation set a general pattern of family ranching that still exists today, although ranching and beef production are rapidly becoming industrialized (Photo 17). Still, there survives the mystique and mythology of the independent family ranch (Photo 19), but small operations are becoming more scarce as large corporations buy up large expanses of land to more efficiently produce meat.

Close on the heels of the cattle industry came the "sodbusters." The Homestead Act of 1862 guaranteed 160 acres of land to anyone who built a house, however modest it may have been, and worked the land for five years. Millions of acres of land were distributed by the Act throughout the West including Colorado. During good precipitation years farming was viable. Many small communities sprang up as service centers to the surrounding farms (Photo 18). During drought periods, some lasting for years, both farms and towns dried up by the hundreds. Most of the farms and farming communities that survived then and survive even now were and are dependent upon supplemental irrigation water from reservoirs or underground aquifers (see Photo 19 again). Vast areas of eastern Colorado are irrigated by intricate and expensive canals, reservoirs, and ditches. Many more acres are irrigated from deep wells into aquifers that are, today, being rapidly depleted. No one knows what the future holds for farming in these dry lands, but water is becoming more scarce and more expensive as farmers now compete with the burgeoning cities for water rights (Photo 32).

Even before Goodnight and Loving traveled northward with their cattle herds, people were using the plains as conduits to places farther west and southwest. Santa Fe, in what is now New Mexico, was founded in 1610, more than a century and a half before our War of Independence. It was under the rule of the Spanish who restricted trade to the north and east even after the United States became a nation. In 1821 Mexico gained its independence from Spain and trade burgeoned. William Becknell first blazed the route that would become the Santa Fe Trail leading from the U.S. into the Mexican territory. The Mountain Branch of the Trail followed the Arkansas and Purgatoire Rivers and then traveled south over Raton Pass. In 1833-34 the Bent brothers, Charles and William, built a "fort" along the route that was part trading post, sanctuary, and rendezvous point. The fort was conscripted by the U.S. Army during the conflict with Mexico and was basically destroyed through misuse to the point where William Bent burned it to the ground. He then moved his operation to a new location fifteen miles to the east. The old fort site has been reconstructed by the National Park Service and is now a National Historic Site commemorating the legacy of the Santa Fe Trail (Photo 22).

SETTLEMENTS AND CITIES

"Pikes Peak or Bust" - the sentiment was inspiring, the geography terrible. The gold rush of 1858 never got within 60 miles of Pikes Peak. The rush to the Pikes Peak region would not occur for another thirty-three years. Colorado's 1858 rush was actually to the mountains and foothills just west of the current site of Denver and in the creeks running in the plains locale of the future city itself. The small mining settlement of Denver was first begun by Kansan Unionists who found "color" in those streams. Simultaneously, several other placer strikes were discovered nearby and produced such mining camps as Auraria, Montana City, and St. Charles. But Denver won out in the struggle to dominate, and by 1867 it was the territorial capital. Denver grew rapidly and steadily and became not only the capital but a railroad town and a manufacturing center. Gates Rubber Company, for example, established its national plant here in 1914.

Denver has a long, storied, and complex history, but two more recent events have defined the cityscapes of Denver at the turn of the 21st century. The first of these was the oil boom of the 1970s and early 1980s. Building in downtown Denver was almost manic at this time with numerous high rise buildings going up, seemingly, overnight (Photo 26). The boom crashed unceremoniously in the 1980s as OPEC's stranglehold on world oil prices vanished and as major decisions by oil companies drastically affected the city's fortunes. The most telling harbinger of bust was when Exxon closed its multi-billion dollar gamble on oil shale development in the Piceance Basin of northwestern Colorado on May 2, 1982. Denver has since recovered from that bust and is again booming. The most vital evidence of this is the phenomenal redevelopment of LoDo (lower downtown) with the cornerstone being the Colorado Rockies' Coors Field (Photo 27). The second event, or more accurately trend, was urban sprawl. Suburbs became the residential communities of choice over the last thirty to forty years. Not only in Denver, but in all of the Front Range communities, the sprawl of the tract homes and the extensive development of "cheap" land produced an ever more expansive and dominant urban form (Photo 31).

Denver, of course, is not the only urban area on the plains of Colorado. Geographers talk about site and situation for the location of places. Site being the exact spot where a place is, and situation being its relationship to places around it. The relatively flat terrain along the western plains next to the mountains provided the situation for the development of railroads and roads - those things that link one place to another. Things like the streams and rivers emanating from the mountains and easy access to mountain resources without the actual rigor of living in the mountains provided optimal sites. In fact this strip of flat land along the mountains is now officially called the "Front Range Urban Corridor" - from Ft. Collins in the north through Loveland, Longmont, Boulder, Denver, Castle Rock, Colorado Springs, Pueblo, and beyond. Each of these cities and urban areas has its own story. Ft. Collins and Boulder, for example, have become "university towns" with all that it entails (Photo 29). Neither of these cities is now just a university town; each has developed its own special economy, and both are vibrant and attractive places to live.

Colorado Springs has its own unique pedigree. It started as a spa town created by Civil War General William Palmer, the builder and owner of the Denver and Rio Grande Railroad. He loved the climate and the site of the place just below the heights of Pikes Peak (Photo 28). He established the city in 1871, but it boomed only after the gold strikes in Cripple Creek, just to the west of Pikes Peak, in 1894. The Cripple Creek strike was one of the richest in the world and built much of what is grand in Colorado Springs. World War II ushered in the military influence that is still strong today.

Camp (Ft.) Carson was the first installation followed by the United States Air Force Academy, Ent Air Force Base, the North American Air Defense Command (NORAD), and the Consolidated Space Operations Center at Schriever Air Force Base. Palmer planned a beautiful central city with broad boulevards, numerous parks, and classical city design. That vision has sadly been superceded by the same urban sprawl evident all along the Front Range corridor.

Pueblo, too, has a very unique lineage. General Palmer was a railroad magnate bent on expanding his influence to both the south and the west. To do so he needed steel for his rails. Colorado was far from the eastern steel centers, so Palmer built his own steel mill - the Colorado Coal and Iron Company that became the Colorado Fuel and Iron Company (CF&I). He put the plant south of the Springs by about 40 miles in what became Pueblo (Photo 30). Abundant water, coal, and iron ore were within relatively close proximity and the Arkansas River was already established as a crossroads of transport both along the Front Range and into the mountains even before CF&I. Steel became the base for Pueblo to become a vibrant and industrialized city. Other towns along the Front Range to the south of Pueblo were also part of the Palmer Empire. Walsenburg and Trinidad and other, smaller settlements became the coal mining centers that fueled the steam coal and steel industries. Pueblo was not immune to the militarization of the area. The open plains northeast of the city were just the type of isolated place that the War Department of World War II liked to put ordinance storage facilities. The result was the Pueblo Army Depot with its regimented bunkers parading to the horizon (Photo 34).

Denver became the capital; Boulder got the university; Cañon City considered itself lucky when it got the Territorial Prison even before Colorado was a state. In Colorado, as in many other states, prisons have recently become a growth industry. Cañon City now boasts several state prisons including the original "Old Max." The prison industry has also been a boom to other towns all over the state, but the biggest penal prize of all belongs to the small town of Florence just down the road from Cañon City. The newest and highest security prison belonging to the Federal Government was recently built here (Photo 33). You can probably guess who some of the residents currently are.

Epilogue

The eastern, high plains of Colorado have at least one schizophrenic characteristic. They possess places as lonely and isolated as any in the state, maybe in the entire West. You can be 50 miles from any town or human habitation. At the same time these plains are where the densest urban development in the state has occurred. Two-thirds of the state's population lives in the ten counties along the Front Range. With this population growth comes things such as the insatiable need for water in an environment that has little of that commodity. This means that over 2.5 million people, and rising fast, have chosen to live and work in the same environment that cannot support individual farm families during extended drought. The two juxtaposed images make an intriguing and often conflicting picture of human settlement in Colorado.

PHOTO 13 The plains of eastern Colorado are not an unwavering expanse of sameness. They exhibit tremendous variety in landforms and ecosystems. This scene in Weld County shows the contrasts between naturally occurring dry lands, more verdant valley bottoms, and irrigated farmlands. The plains of Colorado are many things, but they are not a monotonous landscape. They are places of solitude, beauty, and expansive vistas.

PHOTO 14 The special light following a spring thunderstorm, the dry grass prairie environment, and the geometry of human occupation give this view near Avondale an otherworldly look.

PHOTO 15 Fire has always been a part of the ecosystems of the grasslands. Grasses, with their biomass mostly underground, are not only able to survive fire, but flourish in its aftermath. Humans have adopted fire for their own purposes on the eastern plains. Here we see a field afire to clear the way for new crops to be planted.

PHOTO 16 The riparian ecosystems following streams and surrounding lakes in eastern Colorado are the site of the most densely populated ecosystems on the plains. These thin strips of greenery seen here along the South Platte near Ft. Morgan provide food, shelter, and water for a large number of species of both flora and fauna. Riparian areas are invaluable ecosystems in all parts of Colorado, but they lie in stark contrast to the sere landscapes of the plains as if they were green ribbons on a plain brown paper bag.

PHOTO 17 Because ranching has been such a major economic force in the state, stockyards are a logical ancillary economic activity that are commonly found in the region. This stockyard is one of the largest along the Arkansas River in the southeastern part of the state. Solid and liquid wastes as well as offensive odors have put the stockyard industry into a battle for their existence in many areas.

PHOTO 18   Flagler is like so many small communities in the eastern plains of Colorado — its legacy is that of farming and ranching. These small towns live on the economic edge as farm prices hover below production costs and accumulated debt keeps families from prospering. The stark beauty of the plains and a faith that their lifestyle is worthwhile keeps these places alive.

PHOTO 19 This ranch in Lincoln County shows a typical mix of homestead buildings, feedlots, and verdant irrigated fields. Agriculture is a more vibrant economic sector in the northern plains of Colorado because natural precipitation rates are marginally higher, and soils are generally more fertile than in the southeastern plains.

PHOTO 20   The history of the plains of Colorado contains many noble and proud events - it also contains some that stain the good name of the state. One of the worst atrocities ever committed in Colorado was the massacre at Sand Creek where Colonel John Chivington and soldiers of the First Colorado Regiment attacked a peaceful village of Cheyenne men, women, and children on November 29, 1864. No accurate number of those killed was ever made, but at least 100 Indians died and some think the number is much higher. The exact location of the site itself is a matter of heated debate; this photo is along Sand Creek in Kiowa County and may be the true massacre location. It is now a peaceful and bucolic place. The view looks southeast.

PHOTO 21   The story of the plains of Colorado is incomplete without the story of drought, wind, and despair. Thousands of farmers abandoned the land, and hope, in the recurring dry years that plague the high plains of the state. The landscape is littered with the detritus of these once hopeful lives.

PHOTO 22   Bent's Old Fort was a main stopover along the Mountain Route of the Santa Fe Trail. Built in 1833, it was both a supply outpost as well as the center of military activity along the famous route until 1849. The fort that you see now is a reconstruction of the original 'old' fort. It is now a National Historic Site just east of La Junta and is run by the National Park Service.

PHOTO 23 Piñon Canyon is part of the impressive Purgatoire River Canyon land that runs through southeastern Colorado. These canyons put to rest the idea that all of the plains are plain.

PHOTO 24 There are some awe-inspiring views on the prairie. The suns slanting rays give the Pawnee Buttes an eerie and lonely impression. These buttes have been beacons for navigation for peoples of the plains since time began.

PHOTO 25   Because of the devastation of the 'Dust Bowl' years in the eastern plains of Colorado, the Federal Government set up the National Grassland Program. Colorado has two National Grasslands - the Comanche National Grasslands in southeastern Colorado and the Pawnee National Grassland named after these Pawnee Buttes in the northeastern plains of the state.

PHOTO 26   Much of the Denver skyline was built during the heady days of energy development in Colorado in the 1980s. Energy price declines and the Savings and Loan crisis put a real dent in the development of downtown Denver for several years. The city has weathered that storm and is now again a vibrant and growing urban center - some would even say a boomtown at the foot of the Rockies.

PHOTO 27   One of the signs of the renewed vibrancy of Denver is the massive redevelopment of the lower downtown ("LoDo") spurred in part by the building of Coors Field for the Colorado Rockies. The field, shown here in June of 1996, is one of the most captivating athletic venues in the United States. Some say it is the most beautiful baseball field anywhere. The Rockies won this wild one against the Atlanta Braves 13 to 12.

PHOTO 28   General William Palmer chose this site for his city of Colorado Springs because of its situation. Nestled below the looming slopes of Pikes Peak, the downtown area still has the feel of a small, resort city. This view belies the urban sprawl that stretches for miles to the east and north. The low density of residential and commercial neighborhoods makes Colorado Springs one of the largest by area of the cities in the West.

PHOTO 29   Denver became the capital of the state of Colorado, Cañon City got the prison, and Boulder was left with only the university. Since those days in the 1870s, the University of Colorado at Boulder has grown to be one of the most beautiful campuses in the United States, and it has become one of the premier state universities in the country. The backdrop of the Flatirons highlights the city's site at the foot of the Front Range.

PHOTO 30   Pueblo's economic heritage derives from a railroad mogul of the late nineteenth century - General William Palmer. General Palmer was the owner of the Denver Rio Grande Railroad that opened up much of Colorado. He was also the founder of Colorado Springs. He built a steel mill to make his rails in Pueblo, then a town 40 miles to the south of his "Newport in the Rockies." Water, iron ore, coal and limestone were all readily available near Pueblo – making it a "natural" for steel production.

PHOTO 31   The pattern of modern suburban, residential development is unmistakable in this scene in the Denver suburbs. Straight streets are a rare commodity but fences are *de rigueur* for "making good neighbors."

PHOTO 32   The Pueblo Reservoir is like many bodies of water in Colorado - it is not a natural lake and it has multiple uses. The reservoir has become a significant recreational facility for boaters and anglers, but its main economic importance is for irrigation of crops. Some of the water in the Arkansas River that feeds the reservoir is now being purchased from the irrigators for use by the ever-growing cities along the Front Range. Colorado Springs and Aurora are two of the municipalities purchasing water rights from the farmers of the valley. This photograph illustrates another urban phenomenon that is pulling land out of farm production - this is the growth of suburban ranchettes. The one to five acre lots to the north of the reservoir are good examples of the extensive use of land by many single-family home developments. This view looks northwest to Pikes Peak.

PHOTO 33 Prisons are becoming more and more a part of the cultural landscape of Colorado. A few decades ago only Cañon City had any significant prison population. Now towns including Sterling, Ordway, Buena Vista, Limon, and Delta are homes to state prisons and detention centers. The federal prison here in Florence is one of the most notorious, maximum-security prisons in the country. This facility now holds many of the highest profile federal inmates in the country. This view looks north to Pikes Peak.

PHOTO 34   The plains just east of the Front Range have also been the site of major development by the Department of Defense since the beginning of World War II. The Rocky Mountain Arsenal in Denver; Ft. Carson, Peterson Air Force Base, and the Air Force Academy in Colorado Springs; and the regimented rows of munitions bunkers here at the Pueblo Army Depot are just the most obvious.

Giant thunderstorm cells prowl the plains of eastern Las Animas County. These strong spring and summer storms are a vital ingredient of the plains ecosystem.

Chapter 3

FOOTHILLS

Nature's Formidable Gateway

(5,500 FEET TO 8,000 FEET)

oothills seems like such a small, ill-descriptive word. It conjures up visions of minor bumps in the land, something on the order of topographic molehills. But in Colorado reality, at least, the foothills are much more than merely incidental landscape irregularities. Here foothills are the abrupt, often massive, first vertical impressions we get as we travel westward over the plains. Those hogbacks that create the backdrops of Boulder (Photo 35), Denver, Ft. Collins, or Colorado Springs are anything but molehills. They are, instead, our introduction to the land of high elevations where the landscape's altitude increases a hundred-fold faster than the imperceptible slopes crossed as one travels from Kansas to Denver.

These foothills are also more than just dramatic increases in elevation. They are truly significant "transition zones" between the plains and the mountains in almost every natural sense of the term (Photo 36). Ecosystems change abruptly, often in just a few feet from plains life zone examples to a varied collection of montane life zone communities. Fauna change just as rapidly although they move between ecosystems and adjacent life zones with amazing ease. Weather and climate transform palpably with seemingly minor increases or decreases in elevation. The geology and landforms quickly go from soil-covered, horizontal sedimentary beds to exposed rocks with a decidedly vertical dimension. In a real sense the foothills life zone is a major gateway from the planer plains to the perpendicular world of the mountains. In fact humans have named many of the natural and cultural features within the foothills using the "gateway" expression. Colorado Springs has the Gateway Rocks in the Garden of the Gods; Golden, the small city just west of Denver, was originally called Golden Gate; and, Golden Gate Canyon State Park sits in transition between plains and peaks along State Highway 46 running from Golden to the Peak to Peak Highway - a scenic byway that could define the Montane life zone (see Chapter 4) of the Front Range.

NATURAL TRANSITIONS

The most dramatic of the physical landscape features of the foothills life zone is undoubtedly the hogbacks and flatirons of sedimentary rock so visible along much of the Front Range. Over the eons and with each cycle of mountain uplift, erosion, and deposition, these sedimentary layers were veneered one on top of the previous one. Some were deposited in marine lagoons, some as ancient sand dunes or shoreline beaches, and others were the detrital remains of the sequence of mountain systems which have had Colorado as their home. As each of the mountain uplifts or orogenies occurred, the new mountains were immediately and relentlessly attacked by erosion. Grain by mineral grain, the mountains were made low and the mostly flat-lying sediments were built up. During the recent round of mountain building, called the Laramide Orogeny, these sedimentary rocks, which were lying like a deck of cards, were pushed up by the rising rock of the new mountains. Out in the plains away from the most strenuous uplift, the sedimentary rocks remained relatively flat. But where the intense and localized pressures were great, the sediments were arched up like the edges of that deck of cards being shuffled (Photo 39). They, of course, shattered in many places and this broken rock was itself eroded over time. In other places the mountain building

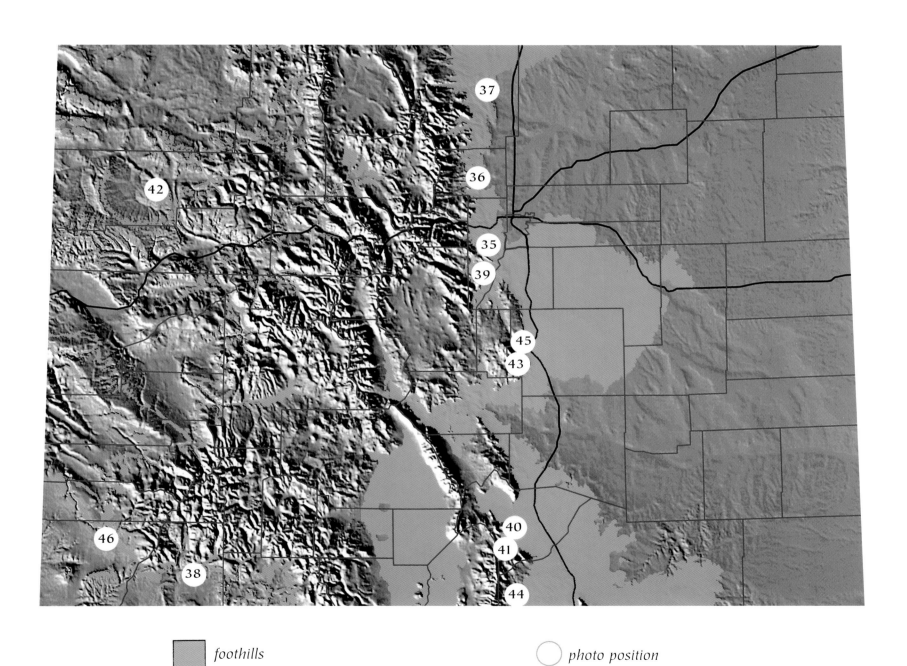

foothills

photo position

pressures bent the sedimentary rock so that their layers or strata were at high angles, often nearly vertical.

Some of the best examples of these extraordinary forces can be seen at the Garden of the Gods in Colorado Springs. Here portions of the Fountain and Lyons formations were both pushed to the perpendicular and beyond. The Lyons produces the tallest and most impressive formation in the Garden. Other places along the foothills that are particularly impressive are the Red Rocks near Morrison, the Flatirons of Boulder, and several hogbacks north and west of Ft. Collins. Somewhat less dramatic examples exist along the Front Range all the way from the Wyoming border to Cañon City, along the Wet Mountain front from Florence to Greenhorn Mountain, and in the foothills of the Spanish Peaks of southern Colorado (Photo 44). Incidentally, the Spanish Peaks region adds another special characteristic to the foothills not seen elsewhere in Colorado. The unique volcanic nature of these two mountains has also produced some of the world's best examples of volcanic dikes radiating out from the mountain cores. Nearly every text on introductory geology includes these features as the quintessential volcanic dikes in existence.

Because the sedimentary rocks were so varied, the exposures of these rocks along the mountain fronts create a complex of different rock and soil types. In addition there are the intruded rocks of the mountains themselves and the complicated fracturing and faulting that went with all of this geologic activity. This overwhelming variation produces an elaborate environment for plants and animals. Probably no where else in Colorado does one get the rapidly changing and mix of environments that we see in the foothills (Photo 42).

In addition to the geologic and landform diversity, climatic changes in the foothills are also abrupt, localized, and frequent. At least two things cause the climate and weather to vary so much in the foothills. First, the foothills life zone is one of the most vertical landscapes in Colorado. The abrupt changes in elevation produce abrupt changes in temperature and humidity. When moving air is forced up the foothills slopes, it cools and the relative humidity increases - this causes overall precipitation also to increase. At the same time if moving air is forced down the slopes, it is "dried out" and keeps precipitation from occurring. The second cause of the climate/weather variation is the impact of "aspect." Aspect is the direction that a landform faces. For example if the slope or side of a mountain faces south, it will receive much more intense sunshine than if the slope faces north even if it is at the same elevation. Over the long term this means the effective or usable precipitation will be lower and temperatures will be higher on south facing slopes. This phenomenon occurs throughout the mountains, but the effects are more pronounced in the foothills where there is also the major transition from plains climates to mountain climates.

THE ECOSYETERS

The diversity of the landforms combined with the variability of the weather and climate of the foothills produces one of the most complex environments in Colorado. There are numerous ecosystems that exist in the foothills - some are the same as plains ecosystems, some are those found in the montane life zone, and some are particularly foothills. The possible ecosystems in this life zone are more abundant than in any other life zone in the state. In some sites you may get plains grassland or plains riparian ecosystems; in others you may find the ponderosa pine, aspen, mountain riparian, or even Douglas fir ecosystems of the montane (Photo 40); and still in others you can get large tracts of piñon-juniper woodlands more commonly associated with the Upper Sonoran life zone (Photo 38).

The most singularly foothills ecosystem, however, is the shrublands ecosystem dominated by scrub oak (Gambel oak in most cases) (Photo 46), along with mountain mahogany, wax currant, skunkbush, chokecherry, and others. Gambel oak and mountain mahogany are often found together in this life zone. They are each interesting and important plants in the shrub ecosystem. Mountain mahogany, for instance, has a root system with filaments of bacteria that fix nitrogen that is then available to other plant species. The seeds from the mountain mahogany are unique in that they are "hairy" spirals that fall with the seed end down and screw themselves into the soil as they dry out. The Gambel oak is a tough and useful shrub. It has several techniques to reduce water loss and use and is tolerant of the very high temperatures possible in the foothills during the summer. Gambel oak also reproduces readily using the hundreds of buds on the roots or lignotubers of the plant. If there is a disturbance of the vegetation, like a fire, these buds are stimulated and re-growth of the Gambel oak begins immediately. The acorns from the Gambel oak are a food mainstay for several animals of the foothills especially the mule deer. Aesthetically, the bright reds and oranges of this ecosystem are one of the highlights of autumn in the foothills.

HUMAN TRANSITIONS

Although travel across the plains was mostly made on established trails (the Santa Fe Trail for instance) in the past or on modern roadways today, there was little in the way of natural barriers to movement over the land. That is not the case for the mountains of Colorado. The term "gateway" is a metaphor for the foothills because it is an apt description of reality. There were only a few usable places where the formidable front of the mountains could be breached by human travel. These gateways were almost exclusively up the streams that had valleys wide enough to accommodate foot traffic, horses, and eventually wagons, trains, and automobiles. Many of these portals to the mountains today are marked by small to medium size towns that were all established on the banks of these streams. La Veta near the Spanish Peaks sits on the Cucharas River; Rye is in Greenhorn Creek valley; Cañon City sits along the Arkansas River; Manitou Springs straddles Fountain Creek; Golden lies on well-known Clear Creek; and Lyons, northwest of Boulder, is on St. Vrain Creek. The openings in the mountain front made by the incessant work of running water are the only places where humans could traverse the initially steep slopes at the beginning of the Southern Rocky Mountains.

The earliest known use of the foothills' access to the mountains was documented in

1924 when Folsom people artifacts were found along the Cache la Poudre River near Ft. Collins (Photo 37). Radiocarbon dates and fluting patterns on projectile points place the date for these artifacts at over 10,000 years ago. From that time in the ancient past until the late 19th century, Native Americans had used these access points to and from the mountains. Utes, the most dominant mountain tribe, Arapaho, Cheyenne, and other plains tribes and clans used these gaps as conduits between mountain and prairie.

Fur trappers and traders were probably the first people of European descent to access the mountains through the foothills corridors. They had little lasting impact except for their devastation of the fur bearing animals, especially the beaver. Historically more significant were the explorers who passed through the area's foothills. Zebulon Pike's expedition (1806) spent time in the foothills of Pikes Peak and the southern mountains of the state; Stephen Long brushed past the foothills as he traveled along the plains just east of the mountains in 1820; and John Charles Fremont made several forays (1843-44, 1845, 1848-49, and 1853-54) into and through the foothills life zone. Fremont, in particular, made significant contributions to the study of the natural history of the area. His extensive journals are still used today to study the landscapes encountered by his expeditions in the mid-19th century.

Permanent settlement in the foothills life zone, however, only began with the rush for riches that was marked by the "Pikes Peak or Bust" gold rush to the area west of Denver (see Chapter 2). Little of value was actually found in the foothills zone itself, but the rush brought people who saw the potential of the land, and they stayed. In the semi-arid environment of eastern Colorado, the water in the streams of these gateways was viewed with enthusiasm. Although the potential for the use of waterpower is not insignificant, there has been little development of that aspect of these streams. But the water was and is coveted for other reasons. Many of the small settlements of the foothills, for instance, are farming communities. Any flat land available was cultivated and the conveniently close water

was used for irrigation (Photo 41). Foothills communities that rely on farming abound: La Veta, Rye, Gardner, Wetmore, and Lyons are but a few. Water in these streams is also desired by the nearby urban areas, especially today when population growth is exploding.

A few efforts have been made to use the resources of the foothills for industrial purposes. One of these is the quarrying industry for stone and rock products that can be gotten from the sedimentary rocks described above. The most notable example is probably the mining of the Lyons sandstone near the town of Lyons. This flat, red, and attractive stone can be seen all over the state in stone walls, landscaped gardens, and buildings. Almost all of the buildings at the University of Colorado at Boulder, for example, are faced with Lyons sandstone. This helps make the Boulder campus one of the most handsome large-university campuses in the country. Another industrial use of the foothills resources is in Golden. A most recognizable beer brand and family name uses the "Rocky Mountain water" in its brewing and especially in its advertising. Coors is synonymous with Golden and the waters that flow there. Lastly, an industry that is booming in Colorado is tourism. Examples of tourist attractions abound in the state including in the foothills. Manitou Springs (Photo 43), for instance, is a tourist mecca that only comes alive during the short tourist season of May through September. Without tourism Manitou and other foothills towns would not thrive.

Epilogue

It is not an accident that many, many parks and open spaces belonging to the state and the cities sitting along the Front Range are in the foothills. First, the foothills are easily accessible to the burgeoning urban populations who live only a few miles to the east. But without the beauty and the stark and alluring landscapes of the foothills, the density of parklands would be considerably less. Some of the most spectacular lands in the foothills are in these parks and almost all of these are due to the geologic legacy of the region. Chatauqua Park in Boulder; Lory State Park in Ft. Collins; Roxborough State Park in Douglas

County; the Garden of the Gods (Photo 45) and Palmer Parks in Colorado Springs; and Pueblo Mountain Park near Beulah are all there because of the unfathomable forces of nature that uplifted our mountains. The foothills life zone is, by far, the least expansive of the life zones in Colorado, but it is also one of the most important and used natural areas we possess.

PHOTO 35   The Red Rocks, near Morrison, are the quintessential hogbacks that help define the foothills lifezone. The natural amphitheater here has been the site of many performances by famous groups over the decades. The tilt of the rocks comes from the tectonic uplifts of the Rocky Mountains eons ago.

PHOTO 36 Bear Canyon just west of the National Center for Atmospheric Research in the foothills in Boulder is an example of a stream-cut valley through the hogbacks. These valleys often became the passes through which people moved into the mountains to the west.

PHOTO 37 The Cache la Poudre River leaves the mountains just north of Fort Collins. This gap in the mountain front has been used by travelers for the last 10,000 years. Evidence of Folsom projectile points have been found near here.

PHOTO 38   Many of the larger towns and cities of the Front Range have encroached over time into parts of the foothills. The same thing has occurred here in Durango where the city lies along the Animas River but also is in a piñon-juniper woodland area as well as scrub ecosystems distinctive of the foothills zone.

PHOTO 39   The dip of these hogbacks in Roxborough Park, just southwest of Denver, is not as severe as that for the Red Rocks near Morrison nor the Flatirons near Boulder. A fault running north/south just west (left) of these hogbacks is partially responsible for this difference in dip angle.

PHOTO 40 Foothills ecosystems are often very complex and intermingled. This area on Cuchara Pass, near La Veta, is a mosaic of grasslands, shrubs, ponderosa pine, and riparian areas. Small changes in elevation and/or aspect help to create the microenvironments responsible for these rapid changes. This photo shows Colorado Highway 160 passing through a gap in the arkosic sandstone "stonewall." The southern Sangre de Cristo Range is in the distance.

PHOTO 41 Some of the foothills areas are good for farming and ranching. Water flowing from the nearby mountains is often available for irrigation of crops and pastureland. These horses are taking advantage of new growth in the spring on a pasture in the foothills near La Veta.

PHOTO 42   Foothills on the western side of the state are often more subtle than those on the eastern side. But the dramatic contrasts just slight elevation changes create can easily be seen here in the Piceance Valley west of Rio Blanco. The lush flat-bottomed valley and meandering stream sit in stark contrast to the foothills on either side.

PHOTO 43 This photo is taken high above Cascade - a small community along Ute Pass, which connects Colorado Springs with the mountains. Manitou Springs is the spa town located just as the pass exits from the mountains. The gateway nature of Manitou is certainly evident from this point of view.

PHOTO 44   The foothills along the southern flanks of the Rockies are more complex than those from Colorado Springs north. Here the "Stonewall" of sandstone lies between the high mountains of the Spanish Peaks and the Sangre de Cristos. The Stonewall is often confused with the radial system of volcanic dikes that radiate out from each of the East and West Spanish Peaks.

PHOTO 45   This view toward the north shows the drama of the Garden of the Gods in Colorado Springs. It also gives you a good feel for the ancient uplift of the mountains to the west (left) that bent these sedimentary beds into an imposing "wall" of rock.

PHOTO 46 Aspen are not the only vegetation that gives vibrant colors in the autumn. Scrub oak on both the eastern and western foothills gives us some of the most striking colors for the fall. These oaks near Dolores are a mélange of yellows, oranges, reds, and greens.

The first breath of coming winter has frosted these fir trees on Banded Peak, on the Continental Divide, Archuleta County.

Chapter 4

MONTANE

finally, we have reached the real high country of Colorado - the mountains. Whenever Colorado comes to mind for residents and non-residents alike, it is the mountains that they inevitably visualize (Photo 63). The frequently forested slopes of the montane life zone rise to elevations of 9,500 feet or more. At these altitudes the land receives both a usually adequate supply of moisture, often in the forms of summer thunderstorms and winter snowpack, and average temperatures high enough to encourage healthy and extensive stands of coniferous trees. But as we look more closely at the montane, we see a life zone that defies simple categories. The expansive forests are there but so are the high, dry grasslands of the four great mountain "parks" (Photo 52), extensive sage brushlands of the western slope, and lush mountain meadows. Although water for all of these various ecosystems is normally adequate, if not overly plentiful, intermittent drought makes wildfire one of the most important natural influences in the montane. For humans much of the montane is relatively

Montane means "of the mountain"

(7,500 FEET TO 9,500 FEET)

inaccessible, yet there is a profusion of small, vibrant communities that, in many cases, are more viable now than in their heyday as mining camps. The montane is many things to many people; but to all of us, it is the start of the quintessential Colorado - the fabled mountains of the Rockies.

THE ECOSYSTEMS

The montane is a generally forested life zone that contains a good number of forest ecosystems. Two of these forest types really define the zone: the Douglas fir ecosystem and the ponderosa pine. One of the most attractive trees in the Colorado mountains is the Douglas fir. The mature Douglas fir is a majestic and regal tree with a full, yet tapered canopy. The beautiful shape of the Douglas is the reason it is so sought after for Christmas trees every December. The soft, almost succulent needles give it a friendly feel, and the distinctive cones are easily recognized with their "snake tongue" or three-pronged bract protruding from beneath the cone scales. The Douglas fir of the Pacific Northwest are massive trees that are coveted for lumber. They can grow to prodigious size; the diameter of one of these giants easily can reach ten feet!

But the Colorado version of the Douglas fir is a much more modest tree. Here the tree is limited by colder temperatures and considerably less moisture. In fact the Douglas firs of Colorado are often right at their limits of tolerance for normal growth. Because they are right at the edge ecologically, the size and distribution of these trees can be affected by seemingly small variations in local climate caused by minor topographic permutations such as a slight change in the hillside aspect. For example north-facing slopes receive less direct sunshine and, therefore, retain somewhat more moisture. On more southerly exposures, the Douglas fir cannot compete with the more drought resistant ponderosa pine or even Gambel oak at lower elevations.

Even more than the Douglas fir, the ponderosa pine is synonymous with the montane. These long-needled pines cover large areas of the life zone. Their rounded crowns and, in mature ponderosa forests, open and scattered distribution makes this a very distinctive forest. The mature ponderosa forest will have a park-like look with widely spaced trees interspersed with grasses and other undergrowth. This is the most stable and healthy form for the trees

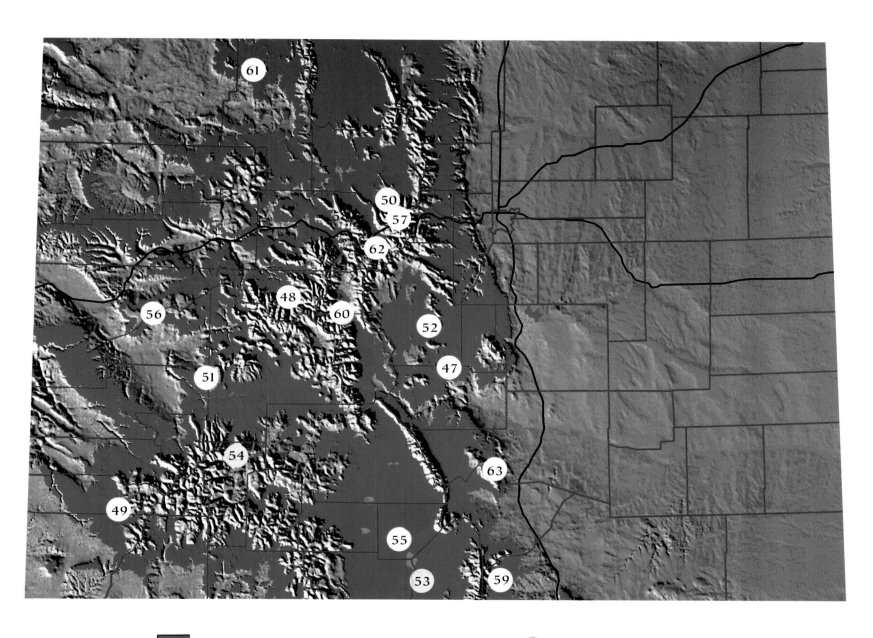

montane

photo position

because it makes it difficult for pathogens to spread from tree to tree. Unfortunately, intervention by humans has caused serious damage to the natural growth patterns of the ponderosa pine ecosystem in Colorado and the entire West.

Fire is a necessary and beneficial part of the natural world. Frequent, low intensity fires are particularly essential to the ponderosa pine ecosystem. Ponderosa are shade-intolerant trees that like open sun and cannot develop to their full potential if growing in the shade of surrounding trees. Low intensity, ground-hugging fires clear out competing vegetation, and many ponderosa seedlings, and keep the more mature trees free from competition for sunlight. The thick bark on the older trees protects them from harm by these relatively low temperature fires. Because of many factors, humans have eliminated most wildfires over the last century or so and have inadvertently allowed densely packed stands of ponderosa to develop. Many, many ponderosa stands today are only marginally healthy or are in severe decline because of this fire control. When fires do occur now, they often become very hot crown fires that destroy all the trees in a stand. Not only are the ponderosas destroyed by the infrequent, large fires, they are much more susceptible to disease. The mountain pine beetle has devastated large stands of ponderosa pine throughout the state over the last few decades. This particular beetle spreads a fungus to the trees which clogs the sap channels of the tree and eventually kills it. The closer the ponderosa pines are together, the easier it is for the beetles to spread their fungal cargo. This small pest has changed the face of the montane life zone over large segments of the state's mountains.

A healthy stand of mature ponderosa pine is a beautiful thing to behold (Photo 59). The large trees stand spread over golden grasses in a bucolic and gentle scene. Better forest management through activities such as prescribed burns tries to recreate some of this natural balance. There is still much work to do to restore the vibrancy of the ponderosa and other ecosystems, but at least most of the ecological connections between fire and ecosystem health are now recognized.

Nature is a wondrously complex thing. Given almost the exact same environmental conditions, nature can devise a wide variety of vegetation communities that could fit those same conditions. A Colorado example of this phenomenon is the western slope areas where the ponderosa pine could or should be located ecologically. The ponderosa pine is missing, however, from much of its normal ecological zone on the western slope. Many of the areas that should be covered in ponderosa in the western reaches of the mountains, given the environmental characteristics, are actually covered by expansive sage shrublands (Photo 61). These sage and grass covered areas account for a good portion of the available grazing lands that entice ranchers to the montane on the western slope.

Another common tree of the montane on both the eastern and western slopes, the lodgepole pine, depends on fire even more than the ponderosa does. In fact the lodgepole pine forest is often called the "fire forest." The cones of the lodgepole display a characteristic called serotony that means that the seeds in the cones are not released or dispersed until the cones are subjected to high temperatures - in other words they need fire. Fire melts the resins in the cone, and the individual seeds are ejected. Not all of the cones of the lodgepole are serotonous, and some ecologists feel that the tree has adapted to various reproductive strategies. But serotony is the dominant seed characteristic for the tree.

Lodgepole pine stands are very homogeneous and species poor — these stands are almost sterile in terms of fauna and other flora. The stands are almost always of the same aged trees that may be growing very tightly packed. Some estimates have the most densely packed stands at well over 10,000 trees per acre, and all the trees will be the same size, shape, and age. These dense collections are often referred to a "doghair" forests, and it is very difficult even to walk through them. Because the lodgepole are shade intolerant trees, smaller and younger trees have little chance to compete with the already established stand. From afar the lodgepole pine look like one vast, olive-green patch of vegetation.

These three forest ecosystems, of course, are not the only ecosystems in the montane. Numerous others, such as the aspen (Photo 47) (see Chapter 5), mountain riparian, mountain meadow, and dry grasslands thrive in certain parts of the life zone. Some of these other ecosystems will be discussed in the mountain parks section below.

THE GEOLOGY AND COLORADO HISTORY

The geology of the montane is both deceptively simple and intensely complex. For much of the Southern Rocky Mountains, the basement rock and the core of the mountains is intrusive rock, mostly granite or granite-like. This core is very old and predates most of the other rock formations in the state. During the episodic mountain uplifts over the eons, this hard and ancient rock was pushed up by unfathomable energy, and it arched the overlying rock burden. Each mountain building period, called an orogeny by geologists, had its own character, but the general pattern was usually the same (with the exception of the volcanic mountain systems of the state). Sedimentary rock overlying the core was lifted, bent, and continuously eroded away leaving the core intrusives behind. The core erodes too, but it is usually a more resistant rock than the sediments above and, therefore, erodes more slowly. All of this erosion creates sediments that are in turn deposited to eventually become new rock. These cycles have gone on for billions of years and will probably continue to go on for many more billions of years.

The stresses and pressures produced by these recurring episodes of mountain building and erosion caused innumerable cracks in the underlying core rock. Eon after eon, uplift after uplift, large scale jointing and fracturing occurred. These fractures often became conduits for superheated fluids originating deep in the earth. The fluids were commonly saturated with minerals, and as the water in the fluids evaporated over time, the minerals were left behind. A fifty-mile wide swath that is over 220 miles long lies across Colorado from north of Boulder to Durango. This was an especially important zone of these joints and fractures in Colorado that we now call the "mineralized belt," and many of the state's most productive mining districts lie in this region. The names of these legendary camps read like a "Who's Who" for Colorado mining: Idaho Springs, Central City, Black Hawk, Leadville, Aspen (Photo 48), Breckenridge, Telluride, Silverton, and many more. There are a few exceptions of course. The most lucrative mining district in Colorado and the West, for example, was Cripple Creek that does not lie in the belt. In spite of the outliers like Cripple Creek, Colorado's mineral belt is the place where the myths and realities of 19th century Colorado mountain history got their start.

Many of the mining camps and towns went into deep depression and several became virtual ghost towns in the first half of the 20th century. The economics of mining and the non-renewable character of mineral veins lead to this dramatic and rapid decline in the fortunes of these towns (Photo 49). At times the decline was literally overnight as when the U.S. Congress repealed the Sherman Silver Purchase Act in 1893. The bottom dropped out of government support for silver purchasing and silver mining districts were doomed. Many of these forgotten towns were raised from the economic trash heap by the 20th century forces of tourism, skiing, and the gaming industry. Now when one goes to Breckenridge, for example, you no longer see the aged and rustic elegance of Victorian houses that were built during the mining boom. Many of these buildings are still there, but they have been transformed and are more than likely to be T-shirt shops or ski outfitters than real residences (Photo 62). The ski industry has metamorphosed many of these venerable, yet decrepit, places into modern showcases for "skiing incorporated" (Photo 58) (see Chapter 5). An even more dramatic, and at times total, transformation has occurred in three former mining towns that are not near ski areas.

In 1991 the voters of Colorado approved limited stakes gambling for Black Hawk, Central City (Photos 50 and 57), and Cripple Creek. At the time these three cities were nearly ghost towns in the winter months. Summers were somewhat better with tourism being the economic engine, but all three were slowly dying. Locals and state officials both thought that gambling could infuse needed life into the communities and that the locals would benefit from year-round gaming fever. The three towns succeeded - some would say they were too successful. What started out as small, "mom and pop" gambling rapidly became controlled by huge corporate gaming concerns. Soon parking lots, fern bars, large casinos, and seemingly infinite slot machines filled the land. Taxes and land values soared, and many of the original locals could not or would not stay in the newly redone, *faux* mining camp creations. Today there is scarcely a locally owned or operated casino, and many of the older and historical portions of the towns are gone. Gambling took on a life of its own, and many feel that the newly manufactured "traditions" may be killing the proverbial golden egg-laying goose. Gambling revenues are no longer golden and the towns are bracing for an expected decline.

There is a multitude of interesting and unique places in the montane of Colorado. But three of these deserve special attention because of their uniqueness. The first is the remnants of a geologic event that took place around 1270 AD. Part of Mesa Seco, a few miles east of Lake City, cataclysmically collapsed and flowed downhill for thousands of feet. This earthflow is now called the Slumgullion Slide and is still slowly moving towards Lake San Cristobal which it created when the slide first moved (Photo 54). Because the slide is still moving, it precludes the vegetation from becoming well established. This creates an eerie, present-day landscape that reminds us of the power of nature in our mountains.

The second place that is of particular interest is the Grand Mesa. Colorado is known for many things, but it is not famous for its concentration of lakes. Yet, on the flat, volcanic plateau of the mesa, sit hundreds of beautiful, bountiful lakes. The mesa is capped by volcanic basalts that flowed over the existing and flat-lying sedimentary rocks. The basalt is hard and resistant rock, and this helped keep the mesa from being eaten quickly away by the ever-present and relentless forces of erosion (Photo 56). Because the mesa is at the elevation of the montane, it receives more precipitation that the surrounding land. Because the mesa is relatively flat, the water collects more readily in the numerous small depressions on the mesa top. What we get is a landscape that looks like northern Minnesota but at an elevation of around 10,000 feet.

Lastly, the montane has a significant landscape of erosion as one of its jewels. The Black Canyon of the Gunnison River (Photo 51), flowing on the southern edge of the West Elk Mountains, shows us the power and speed with which erosion can work. The plateau through which the river runs has only been in the process of being uplifted for the last few million years - a blink of an eye in geologic terms. But the force of running water has cut down into the bedrock to a depth of 2,425 feet below the plateau top. The canyon created is one of the deepest and narrowest in North America.

THE PARKS

Another geologic legacy left to the montane life zone of Colorado are the four large, nearly treeless basins or parks that bisect the state's mountains. North, Middle, and South Parks and the San Luis Valley are all geologic structural basins, called grabens by earth scientists, that lie at relatively high elevations within the montane. They are only basins because higher mountains surround these parks and provide a rain-shadow effect for all four of them.

The largest of the parks is the San Luis Valley (Photo 53). It may also be the most interesting, both naturally and culturally. The San Luis Valley is the only true desert in Colorado with precipitation rates averaging from six to eight inches per year. Yet the valley sits on trillions upon trillions of gallons of groundwater in aquifers rising to just below the surface. This groundwater is generated by the large runoff from the bordering San Juan and Sangre de Cristo Mountains. Needless to say, this vast water reserve has been, is now, and will continue to be fought over in the water courts of the state. The valley is also home to the oldest continuously occupied settlement in the state, the small town of San Luis. This is a traditionally Hispanic community which was settled in 1851 to service the growing farm industry that began in that era. The San Luis Valley is also home to several Mormon communities that began immediately after

Brigham Young selected Utah for his people. The valley has various other cultural oddities, especially near the northern valley town of Crestone. This community is home to a Roman Catholic Carmelite monastery, a New Age community, and a Buddhist Karma Kagyu meditation center. The valley also supports an alligator ranch, a mushroom farm, one of the country's largest organic beef operations, a UFO viewing venue, and extensive quinoa fields.

The other three parks are less eccentric, but are still impressive in their own right, both naturally and culturally. Because all of the parks are in the rain shadows of various mountain ranges, they are all victims of low average precipitation rates. The San Luis Valley is the driest, but they all have less than ten to twelve inches of precipitation annually. This means that treed vegetation is at a minimum, and it is replaced by grasslands and dry scrub ecosystems. The flora in these ecosystems varies from the greasewood and four-winged saltbush, indicative of southwestern deserts that we see in the San Luis Valley, to relatively lush grasslands and extensive sagebrush covered lands of Middle and North Parks. Oddly enough, in the midst of these dry places, one can find some of the lushest vegetation in Colorado. In all the parks, but especially in the San Luis Valley (Photo 55) and North Park, there are extensive riparian areas that grow lavishly along streams and rivers. One particularly incongruous environment lies in North Park along the Michigan and Illinois Rivers which rise in the mountains to the east. These rivers take on an anastomosing form, meaning they have many intertwining, permanent channels that spread the river over large areas. This exuberance of water allows lush growth of willows and other riparian species. Because of this extensive habitat, the Colorado Division of Wildlife has reintroduced moose to the area. The moose have flourished amongst the tangles of water and vegetation in the bottom of this, seemingly, dry valley bottom. They are now so numerous that they have begun to emigrate to other areas of the state.

SOME LAND USE QUESTIONS

"35 acres ... meadow and woods"

"Great weather, numerous outdoor recreation opportunities - 35 + acres"

"These spectacular 35 acre ranches are located ..."

"35 acre ranch with fantastic views ..."

All of the above real estate advertisements were taken from the world-wide-web. The key words that were used for the web search were simply "35 acres." These advertisement sound (text) bites all came up promoting 35 acre ranches for sale in the montane of Colorado. These four ads were among hundreds and hundreds of similar promotions that were also found. This illustrates the proliferation of mountain lands in Colorado, mostly in the montane, which are being subdivided by developers, often from larger working ranches that have been sold for more lucrative development.

Traditionally, most of the private land in the montane of Colorado has been used for ranching. Because of the cool temperatures and short growing season, one of the few crops that can be grown here is hay, so farming is not often viable. Successful ranching in Colorado takes very large expanses of land because cattle take up to 50 acres per head to feed using only the natural forage available. Hay meadows, often irrigated, supplement the open grazing on natural vegetation. The majority of the land in the montane of Colorado is held by the federal government - especially the Bureau of Land Management and the U. S. Forest Service. But even this federal land is used by ranchers who lease these public lands for their grazing opportunities.

Ranchers with their roaming herds of cattle and expansive use of the land, have had some detrimental effects on the land. But in the broader view, their relationships with other interests in the montane have been moderately positive. Although there are many documented abuses like overgrazing, usually ranchers and wildlife get along passably, not withstanding the proposed re-introductions of species such as wolves, grizzly bears, and lynx. The development of the 35 acre "ranchette" (they cannot be seriously considered real ranches) has changed the human/wildlife equation.

In 1972 the Colorado legislature passed a law that allowed developers to subdivide their land into 35 acre or greater parcels without any county land use review. Anything smaller than 35 acres was subject to county planning regulations. The wide-ranging impact of the law is becoming clear with the accelerating demand for vacation homes in Colorado. The decline in prices for beef and the general move away from red meat by consumers has put pressure on ranchers to sell their land to real estate developers at ever increasing rates. The montane of Colorado is rapidly becoming a zone of 35 acre parcels complete with house, driveway, fences, and Kentucky blue grass. Where once cattle shared the range with wildlife such as elk, mule deer, and pronghorn, the once open range is now being cut into a patchwork of small landholdings and new roads that restrict the normal movements of the wildlife (Photo 60).

EPILOGUE

In his book *Song of the Dodo*, David Quammen discusses at length the problems inherent in breaking apart and isolating wildlife habitat. He cites examples from around the world of the effects caused by this kind of action. It is yet to be seen what long-term effects this segmentation of lands in Colorado will have. The trend, however, seems to be accelerating; and the genie cannot be put back in the bottle. Only time will tell what the final impacts of the "35 acre" revolution and other mountain development will be for the wildlife that have roamed the montane for thousands of years or for the traditional ranching communities of the mountains.

PHOTO 47 These strikingly hued aspen stands on Thirty-Nine Mile Mountain in Park County are typical of those found throughout the montane and subalpine of Colorado. Thirty-Nine Mile Mountain is a Tertiary period volcano that affected the landscapes of much of the montane west of Pikes Peak.

PHOTO 48 The famous ski town of Aspen lies in the montane but is surrounded by the high subalpine and alpine lands that are used by the ski industry of the state. Aspen was once an almost forgotten mining camp that has grown into the most exclusive city in Colorado. This view looks south towards Independence Pass.

PHOTO 49 Mining has been a huge part of the history and culture of the montane in Colorado. This photo shows the old mining town of Rico in the San Juan Mountains in the southwestern part of the state.

PHOTO 50 Artifacts of the past mining legacy dot the landscapes around the storied town of Central City. The city itself is one of three mountain towns that sport legalized gambling in Colorado. There is little agreement about the wisdom of turning historic mining towns into modern gambling havens.

PHOTO 51   The top of the Black Canyon of the Gunnison is within the montane. The canyon itself is one of the world's deepest (2,425 feet) and narrowest (1,300 feet at its narrowest point). Just recently the Black Canyon of the Gunnison National Monument became a National Park, giving it increased protection and status.

PHOTO 52 Curved ribbons of upturned sedimentary rocks in South Park are accented by the ponderosa pine and aspen growing on these slightly elevated formations. The coarser soil on the sedimentary exposures and slight increases in precipitation give trees a chance in this semi-arid environment. The remainder of the park's relatively flat terrain is mostly covered by sparse grasslands.

PHOTO 53 The San Luis Valley is the largest of the four montane parks in Colorado. It is the most intensively farmed (see the circle irrigation patterns) because of the availability of water in shallow aquifers. Culturally, the valley is a meeting place of older Hispanic cultures and newer Anglo peoples. Blanca Peak and the Sangre de Cristo Range are seen in the distance. The Great Sand Dunes can just be seen nestled between the two.

PHOTO 54 The Slumgullion Slide is one of Colorado's most unique geomorphic landscapes. This mass movement of land first occurred around 1270 AD, but parts of it are still active today. Lake San Cristobal was created by the slide and is the lake for which Lake City is named.

PHOTO 55 The Alamosa Wildlife Refuge in the San Luis Valley is a collage of water and wetlands that lures millions of migrating birds including the well-known sandhill and whooping cranes. The birds, in turn, lure thousands of bird watchers from around the region.

PHOTO 56 Grand Mesa is just at the upper limit of the montane and grades into the subalpine for much of the mesa's extent. The basaltic "cap" of hard rock protects the softer sedimentary rocks below and provides many basins for small lakes. The La Sal Mountains of Southeastern Utah are seen in the far distance.

PHOTO 57   The new artifacts of the gambling industry have transformed Central City into a very different place from its original ideal. Parking lots, false facades, and faux Victorian buildings are now the norm.

PHOTO 58 Dense condominium development crowds a hillside at Silverthorne, in Summit County.

PHOTO 59 Healthy stands of ponderosa pine spread around Monument Lake near the Spanish Peaks (in the background). The "monument" of the lake is the monolith of rock rising from the lake's waters. (Seen in the lake at lower center.)

PHOTO 60 The Twin Lakes near Independence Pass are reservoirs in the water systems of Front Range communities. They were originally natural but have been engineered to increase their storage capacity. Recent land development near the lakes has created a landscape cut by innumerable gravel roads.

PHOTO 61 The area around Steamboat Lake north of Steamboat Springs is a good example of the sage covered montane lands of the western slope. Hahns Peak stands as a backdrop to the lake. The lake is really a reservoir that was built to supplement the water needed at power plants downstream on the Yampa River.

PHOTO 62 The boomtown of Breckenridge is another old mining town that has re-struck it rich with skiing and real estate. Condos are fast replacing the Victorian charm of the early mining era. Growth in the town continues at an accelerating pace.

PHOTO 63 Greenhorn Mountain (the top of which is in the subalpine) is surrounded by the Wet Mountains which are dominantly in the montane. They are "wet" because they are the first mountains to intercept the Gulf of Mexico moisture that comes from the southeast. The town of Rye lies in the foreground.

Stonewall Valley with southern Sangre de Cristo Culebra Range in background, western Las Animas County. This view looks to the southwest.

Chapter 5

S U B A L P I N E

High Mountains and Big Trees

(9,500 FEET TO 12,000 FEET)

Water! No one thing can adequately describe any of the life zones discussed in any of these chapters, but water comes close to defining the essence of the subalpine. Atmospheric physics dictates that as air rises, for example when it is pushed up and over a mountain range, it cools. This cooler air cannot hold as much water vapor as the warmer air below. The water vapor is forced to come out of the vapor-state and condenses to form small droplets of liquid water or crystals of solid water creating clouds. Over time these droplets or crystals grow so large that gravity forces them to fall in the form of rain or snow. In Colorado the alpine (the region above the subalpine) receives by far the most total precipitation, especially in the form of snow (Photo 65) and much of the snow that falls on the alpine is scoured and transported by very strong winter winds. This wind-borne snow collects just below treeline in the high elevations of the subalpine life zone. The result is that a large amount of snow falls in the subalpine — ecologists, in fact, often call the subalpine forest the 'snow forest' for this reason.

This abundance of water means many vital things to the subalpine itself and to other life zones and regions of Colorado and the West. For the western United States, Colorado is the birthplace of rivers. Four of the major rivers of the high plains and the Southwest are born in Colorado — the Platte and Arkansas Rivers flow east through the high plains to feed the Mississippi; the Rio Grande flows south into and through New Mexico, skirts Texas and empties into the Gulf of Mexico; and the Colorado River is the artery of life for human existence for much of the Southwest. Each of these four watercourses is fed, in turn, by a multitude of rivers and streams that either start or get most of their water from the melted snows or the summertime thunderstorms of the subalpine mountains of Colorado. The St. Charles and Purgatoire Rivers flow into the Arkansas; the Cache la Poudre feeds the South Platte; the Alamosa and the Conejos feed the Rio Grande; and, a litany of rivers supply the fabled Colorado including the East, Gunnison, Taylor, Roaring Fork, Blue, Fraser, Crystal, Dolores, San Juan, San Miguel, and *El Rio de las Animas Perdidas* to name a few. In the final accounting these rivers give life to cities and farms and ranches far beyond the borders of Colorado. They are used, some would say used up, by millions of people along their courses and beyond. All water in them is 'allocated,' and by the time they reach their seaward goals, it is virtually gone. Every drop of water in the Platte is estimated to be used eight times before it reaches the Mississippi, and the Colorado often has only dry sand leaving its mouth in Mexico when it empties into the Gulf of California (Photo 72).

SUBALPINE ECOSYSTEMS

But not all of the water from the subalpine flows into the rivers to be taken from the area. The subalpine's multitude of ecosystems have developed as they have because of the gift of water (Photo 75). The subalpine in Colorado spans elevations from around 9,500 feet to about 12,000 feet above sea level. In this altitude range we find a varied mix of ecosystems that seemingly define our high mountain regions. One ecosystem that is small in total size but is profound in impact on the natural world of the mountains is the riparian zone (Photo 71). The riparian zone runs along the banks of the innumerable streams and the shorelines of the many lakes of the subalpine. As

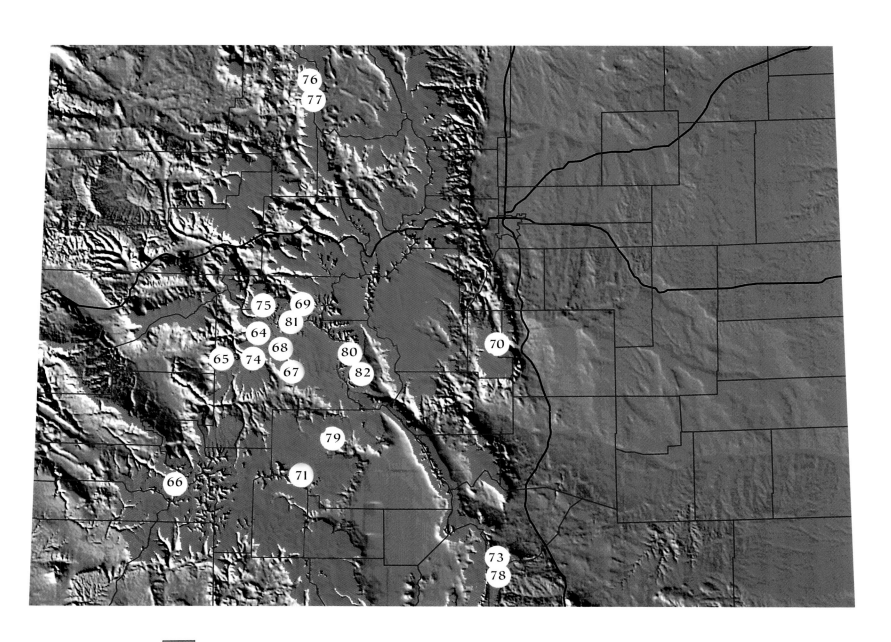

subalpine   ◯ photo position

discussed in the chapter on the plains, it is a diverse and rich ecosystem that is verdant and a prolific giver of life. The dense and varied vegetation in this setting is home to a large number of fauna species. Insects, birds, rodents, predators, and many invertebrates cluster in or near the riparian zone. Shelter, food, and of course water, are all supplied in relative abundance here which encourages the proliferation of life along the watercourses.

The signature forest ecosystem of the subalpine life zone and the one for which the name 'snow forest' was coined is the spruce-fir forest (Photos 67 and 73). This forest constitutes large tracts of Engelmann spruce and subalpine fir (and sometimes a variant of the subalpine fir called the cork-bark fir). These are the tall, statuesque arboreal spires we see in the high mountains. These two tree species make up the large majority of forestland in the subalpine. The trees themselves have evolved perfectly for their role in the snow forest. The sleek and slender trees do not gather or hold large amounts of snow that could overload the branches and break the tree apart. Snow does collect on the branches of these trees but is sloughed off even by gentle breezes. The winds at this elevation are most often not gentle but blow with considerable force, especially in winter. The narrow profile of these trees offers little wind resistance that helps keep the trees from blowing down. Sometimes, on very rare occasions, even the low wind resistance of the trees is not enough to save them. On October 25, 1997 in the Mount Zirkel Wilderness Area of the Park Range to the northeast of Steamboat Springs, a freak weather incident occurred. A single windstorm with hurricane force winds up to 120 miles per hour blew down thirteen thousand acres of spruce-fir forest (Photo 76). Without the inherent ability of the Engelmann spruce and subalpine fir to resist high wind speeds, these kinds of events would occur much more often in the windy realm of the high mountains of Colorado.

The spruce-fir forest of the subalpine is the dominant ecosystem here for many reasons; one of the most important of these is that the two trees are shade-tolerant. In many forest ecosystems, the stands of trees are all of similar age because saplings, shaded from the energy giving sun, cannot compete with the mature trees. Although spruce-fir saplings will do better in open sunlight, they can tolerate shady conditions and they grow slowly and steadily until given the opportunity of a blow-down or other tree-clearing event that may remove the more mature trees. This, seemingly trivial ability actually has profound effects on the long-term viability, and therefore, the longevity of the entire spruce-fir forest. Shade tolerance allows the Engelmann spruces and subalpine firs to keep reproducing and maintain the competitive edge they need to out-compete other flora. Although the long-used term for this is a 'climax' forest or community, the term is in some disfavor with ecologists because of the connotation that the forest will never change. The Mount Zirkel blow-down demonstrates that it obviously can (Photo 77). Contemporary ecologists prefer terms such as 'compositional equilibrium' or 'steady-state' to imply the same concepts as climax but without the air of inevitability involved.

Toward the upper elevation limits of the spruce-fir forest, some environmentally induced changes occur to the trees. Depending upon latitude, sun exposure, slope angle, and other factors, trees cease to grow above certain elevations. Between where trees stop growing tall and upright (timberline) and where trees do not grow at all (treeline or treelimit), there exists a zone we call an ecotone. Ecotone, as used by ecologists, means the transition area between two dominant life zones - in this case between the subalpine and the alpine (Photo 64). See Chapter 6 on the alpine for a discussion of the ecotone.

Although the spruce-fir forests are the most dominant and extensive forest ecosystem of the subalpine, it is the quaking aspen ecosystem that is most cherished, especially by tourists, photographers, and hikers in the autumn. There is no better indicator of the changing seasons in Colorado than the aspen. The lush, almost succulent green buds of the aspen in early spring foretell the sun and warmth to come. In summer the shady, cool stands of aspen are welcomed by hikers like oases in a desert. The golds, oranges, and yellows of autumn aspen just about define that season in the high country. Even the musty smell of aspen dust in the air during the fall triggers nostalgia. And aspen's white bark with its black blemishes is like a surreal picture against the snowy backdrop of winter. The ever-circling seasons in the mountains seem to run by the aspen clock, and a majority of the most sought after aspen groves of Colorado are in the subalpine life zone (Photo 75).

Where the spruce-fir forest is often called the snow forest, the aspen forest could be called the 'disturbance forest,' as is the lodgepole pine forest discussed in the montane life zone chapter. Although there are aspen stands that are now believed to be 'climax' stands, most aspen groves develop in response to some disturbance of the land and are considered a pioneering species. Fire, avalanche, landslide, and more recently, the bulldozer are all stimulants to aspen growth. The key to this rapid pioneering characteristic by aspen is the extensive root system that an aspen has. Each individual aspen has a root network that spreads out just under the soil surface from the original plant (called the 'ortet'). New trees (or tree trunks at least) grow vertically from these roots and are genetic clones of the ortet. These 'mamets' grow in a concentric, expanding zone of ever younger trees out from the central tree. This entire mass of aspen is a single organism and these stands are, not surprisingly, called clones. All the trees in the clone will also be the same sex, have the same general leaf size and serration pattern, and bud at the same time in the spring. The aspen clone exhibits the most dramatic clonal characteristic in the autumn when all trees in a clone will change color at the same time, and the shades of yellow and orange of each tree in the clone will be identical. It is easy to pick out the individual clones during the height of aspen color (Photo 78). Some aspen clones become very large and may cover several acres. There is some considerable scientific justification for classifying the aspen as the largest single organism in the world. The total mass of one of these clones can far exceed that for a blue whale or a sequoia tree, for example.

The aspen root system is also responsible for the pioneering character of aspen. If the above ground portion of the aspen is destroyed by some force, say a large snow avalanche, the roots remain alive, and new growth can begin immediately the following spring. Because aspen are not shade tolerant, aspen groves will usually be invaded and forced out by the expansion of the spruce-fir forest (Photo 79). The clonal root system of the aspen, however, will remain alive and protected underground, maybe for centuries. Some day the spruce-fir forest may be destroyed (by the Mount Zirkel wind storm for example), and the aspen are primed to begin their rapid growth to replace the conifers - and the cycle begins again.

The spruce-fir forest is the snow forest; the aspen forest and the lodgepole pine forest are the disturbance forests. There is one more forest type that can be characterized by a single term, and that is the 'wind forest.' The wind forest is composed of the gnarly limber and bristlecone pine trees. These two species are often seen together or may exist in single-species stands in areas that are repellant to other tree species. Pick the windiest, rockiest, most exposed site in the subalpine and there is a good chance you will find either limber or bristlecone pines. Limber pines are well described by their common name and by their Latin name - *Pinus flexilis*. The limbs of the limber pine are so flexible that they can be tied into knots without harming them. This characteristic gives the limber pine the ability to go-with-the-flow – the flow of wind that is. High winds just make the tree bend and flap around but cannot break the rubbery branches. This suppleness helps the limber pine to out compete other tree species in areas where they might be broken or blown down.

Bristlecone pine trees have almost as much wind tolerance as the limber pine. The bristlecone is also one of the oldest living things in Colorado. The Latin name of species of bristlecone in Colorado is *Pinus aristata* - the aristocratic pine. Some of these trees have been found to be nearly 2,000 years old, and stands with trees over 700 years old are common. As old as the Colorado bristlecones are, they are not the same species of bristlecone which are the real elders of the natural world. Although the *Pinus longaeva* growing in the White Mountains of California may be as old as 4,800

years, the Colorado cousin is still an ancient and venerable tree. Needless to say, these trees grow very slowly. Coring from a bristlecone often reveals growth rings so thin as to be nearly invisible. These tight growth rings actually help the tree fend off insects and other pests. The wood is so dense that it prevents a boring insect from penetrating the tree. The needles of this species also live much longer than those of other conifers; this frees up energy that might go into needle production to be used for survival.

Limber pine can be recognized by its gnarled, yet stately look, its flexible branches, and its five-needle fascicle. Bristlecone pine looks a lot like the limber, but it has sharp bristles on the cones and resin droplets on the five-needle bunches. Both of these tree species deserve our respect for their tenacity in the face of fierce environmental odds and for their longevity in very trying conditions. One of the best, most accessible places to get a close-up view of these trees, especially the bristlecones, is at the Mt. Goliath Natural Area on the road up Mt. Evans west of Denver.

One last ecosystem of the subalpine deserves attention. The summer thunderstorms and melting winter snows provide for lush mountain grasslands and meadows. Often, these open lands are only temporary places that eventually will be replaced by trees. Until that time they provide a resource of high energy, protein rich grazing for wild and domesticated animals alike. Many a rancher leases summer grazing rights to these places from the U. S. Forest Service or the Bureau of Land Management. The cattle industry has come to see these leases as a right of the industry in Colorado. These meadows mean more esthetic things to others. Subalpine meadows produce a vast array of wildflowers that color the landscape as no other ecosystem does. One cannot go hiking through the subalpine meadows of Colorado during June or July without being captivated by the rainbow of colors of the flowery show. A litany of wildflowers is displayed in various combinations in each of these meadows — marsh marigold, sandwort, shrubby cinquefoil, broadleaf arnica, golden aster, Indian paintbrush, fireweed, Parry primrose, shooting

star, lupine, penstemon, sunloving aster, and showy daisy to name only a few. Because of the profusion of flowers in the subalpine, small towns in the life zone have wildflower festivals at about the same rate as small towns on the eastern plains of Colorado have rodeos. Looking at the summer flowers is rapidly becoming a real industry in and of itself.

SKIING

The subalpine, that snow forest zone, is also the place where the Colorado ski industry flourishes. From around the world the typical image of Colorado is white, downy snow covering majestic mountains that are being skied (and more and more snow boarded) by thousands of happy people. This image is at least as much reality as it is myth. A serendipitous mix of factors have come together to make the mountains of Colorado and their ski slopes the envy of much of the world's winter sports set.

Take the mountains as a starting point. Ski slopes require the balancing of two things to be successful. First, the hills must be steep enough to provide the requisite thrill of schussing down them at considerable speed (at least the black diamond slopes do). The excitement, especially for the young or young at heart, is what skiing is about for them. The second requirement is that the slopes are not so steep that the skiing terrain is bordering on treacherous or the snow has a hard time staying in place (see the section on avalanches below). Colorado maintains an almost perfect balance between these two. With only a few exceptions, the ski areas of Colorado have a prodigious mix of advanced and beginner slopes to meet almost all skiing tastes with only a low potential for avalanche activity. For those who seek more dangerous thrills, backcountry or alpine bowl skiing offers steeper slopes but with the added specter of increased avalanche threat.

The most important component of the mix that makes Colorado a great ski state is the snow. The Sierras and the Cascades wring most of the moisture from Pacific storms before they get to Colorado. These western mountains get heavy, wet snowfalls that are often referred to as Cascade or Sierra 'concrete.' Our snow, on the other hand, is usually goose-down light, and Colorado's only competition for the best powder in the country is Utah. The light, almost ephemeral, characteristic of our snow comes from the physics of snow crystals at very high altitudes and low air pressures. At the elevations where our snow is produced inside the clouds, there is little water vapor available. This cold, almost dry air is what produces our white gold — the powder snow of our high mountains. The snow is superb and usually reliable. But to preclude any economic problems with occasional drought years, many of the ski areas are adding artificial snow making to their repertoire. This often puts ski areas in direct conflict with other uses for the water — wildlife habitat, urban water demands, and irrigated agriculture are only the most obvious.

History contributed its part to the serendipity of the Colorado ski industry too. Some skiing in the state has been around since the mining days of the late nineteenth century. Scandinavian miners frequently moved about the mountains on the long, wooden skis so treasured in their native lands. Irwin near Kebler Pass, for example, hosted the first ski competition in the state in 1883. The 1930s brought some rough-hewn slopes in Aspen, and the first chair lift in Colorado was built in Crested Butte in 1939 (Photo 68). But the real catalyst for Colorado skiing was World War II. In 1942 12,000 men came to the quiet valley of the Eagle River at Pando, just north of Tennessee Pass, to begin training for the U. S. Army's Tenth Mountain Division. The Tenth Mountain was to become famous for its record in Italy and for the skill and daring of its troops. After the war thousands of these skilled soldier-skiers remained dedicated to the sport of skiing. They returned to the U.S. with high hopes, energy, and entrepreneurial daring. Many, if not most, of the major ski areas of the country were begun or expanded by these returning veterans. Aspen Mountain, Vail, Steamboat, Arapaho Basin, Buttermilk, Snowmass — the Who's Who of Colorado skiing were all created or rejuvenated by these men (Photo 69). Without World War II the ski industry of Colorado would have eventually grown, but it would not have exploded on the scene nearly as fast or with so much vigor.

Other factors also contribute to making Colorado a skiing mecca. Skies so blue they imprint themselves in your brain, warm temperatures (most of the time) to encourage outdoor activities, and sunny ski slopes all beckon people in numbers only dreamed about in other ski regions. And access to the ski resorts is abundant thanks in large part to the numerous roads built by the nineteenth century mining industry. Add to this the rapid development of airfields around the state that lures the affluent, hurried, and mobile skiing connoisseurs.

AVALANCHES

Although most of the state's ski areas are fairly well protected from snow avalanche activity, Colorado remains the state with the highest avalanche occurrence rate in the country. Each year hundreds to thousands of avalanches run down the slopes of the state's mountains (Photo 80). Usually these snow slides do nothing more than move snow from high up on the slopes to valleys below. They may, of course, uproot some trees (spurring aspen re-growth in the process), but seldom do damage to property or injuries to humans occur. Nonetheless, Colorado remains the state with the highest death toll from avalanches because of the few deadly slides that do take place each winter. These fatal accidents are almost always in the backcountry where extreme skiers, cross-country tourers, or snowmobilers find the solitude and excitement they seek.

The question is often asked - "Why don't they just avoid the avalanche prone slopes?" The answer is not simple and has many components of course, but there are two major contributors to the majority of the problem. First, people go on avalanche slopes because, after all is said and done, that is where to find the best snow and slope difficulty for great backcountry skiing. People weigh the odds of an avalanche occurring while they are on the slope against the adrenaline rush of skiing some of the best places on Earth. Most times they win; sometimes they lose. The second reason is not so cavalier - people are just unaware of the impending dangers of skiing on a particular slope. Often the hidden dangers below the surface of the snow cannot be seen without digging a pit and analyzing the snow below.

Snow is a very ephemeral substance that changes rapidly and continually. One of the most important changes goes by the technical term 'temperature gradient metamorphism.' Snow crystals at the bottom of a snowpack near the ground can experience degradation in their crystalline structure and strength caused by the temperature differential between the air temperature and the ground temperature. If the ground is very warm relative to the air, the crystals regroup in a very fragile form called depth hoar. This hidden, weak layer lies far below the surface of the pristine snow that sparkles so peacefully in the Colorado sunshine, maybe for months. It is waiting for some trigger to release the snow and allow it to slide on the depth hoar. That trigger is often an unsuspecting skier or snowmobiler whose weight collapses the snowpack and sends it down the slope with skier or snowmobiler engulfed. These are, of course, not the only causes of snow avalanche death or injury, but they are major contributors to the problem. Help is available from sources such as the Colorado Avalanche Information Center and the U. S. Weather Bureau. And many avalanches are released intentionally by ski areas and the Colorado Department of Transportation to get them to run while people are out of the way. But when all is finally said, good decision making, good information, and good knowledge of snow characteristics can only reduce the risk of avalanche danger; nothing we can do will eliminate it altogether. That is the nature of snow and mountains.

GLACIAL LANDSCAPES

All landscapes, in particular mountain landscapes, are the result of some level of uplift or depression from one or more sources and subsequent erosional forces. John Wesley Powell, the great nineteenth century explorer/geologist/ethnographer, made the observation that places where erosion is most aggressive are also places that are the highest in elevation. He reasoned correctly that the high potential energy of elevation makes erosion more efficient and effective than land at lower elevations and lower potential energy. Water, the most prodigious worldwide erosion agent, does more overall erosion work than any other phenomenon. But in many of the high mountains of the world, glacial activity over the last two million years has had profound effects on the way the mountain lands look.

Almost all mountain glaciers of Colorado head in the alpine life zone; therefore, the genesis of glaciers will be discussed in that chapter. There are, however, significant glacial landscape features that are evident in the subalpine. One of these is the particular erosional character of alpine or valley glaciers. Unlike water or wind, glaciers are not sensitive to the size or weight of the material they can carry. It matters not a bit to a glacier whether a microscopic clay grain or a boulder the size of a house is being carried by the ice. It all goes. A glacier also has erosive power all along its base, and therefore, valley bottoms get widened and flattened. This creates a very distinctive glacial erosion cross-section — the U-shaped valley (Photo 81). Where glaciers were not present in mountain areas, the valleys cut by flowing water would show the distinctive V-shape cross-section. The difference is obvious in the subalpine of Colorado's mountains (Photo 82).

A second landscape feature is much more subtle than the U-shaped valley. This feature is really a spectrum of characteristics coming from the deposition of the debris carried when the glacier melts. A general term for these deposits is a moraine. Moraines come in many forms — the arcuate end moraine that crosses so many valleys and dams so many lakes; the ground moraine that covers many valley floors and promotes willow growth in the loose, wet soil; and, the lateral moraine that lines the sides of many valleys. Moraines are comprised of a mixed, unsorted jumble of rock and soil debris. They contribute to the legacy of the 'Rocky' Mountains, and their distribution helps determine the pattern of ecosystems in the region. These glacial deposits are ephemeral, at least in the long run. If no new glacial activity occurs over the next million years or so, most glacial landscapes of the subalpine will be reworked by water erosion. For now, glacial erosion and deposition are important contributors to our high mountain landscapes.

MINING

The foundation below all of what we have talked about, of course, is the bedrock geology discussed at length in the montane chapter. The highest elevations in the state, the subalpine and the alpine, are generally the youngest mountains or those with the most resistant rock types. Many of Colorado's metallic mineral resources are found in these same high mountains. Two related phenomena are primarily responsible for this. First, the older rocks, which are mostly ancient igneous intrusions such as granite, have been pushed around and fractured time after time over the eons. The most recent and drastic movement of these rocks took place during the Laramide orogeny, the mountain uplift episode that began about 65 million years ago. Uplift of thousands of feet put all of this rock under tremendous stress and strain that fractured and faulted large segments of the landscape. Mineralized fluids percolated up into these fractures and created the concentrated zones of ore that are now mineable.

The second phenomenon that contributed greatly to the quantity of metallic ore (especially gold and silver) was the Tertiary age volcanic activity in the San Juan Mountains and a few other outlying areas. The major volcanic activity spanned an approximate range from thirty million years ago to twenty million years ago. The San Juans and Cripple Creek are the most prominent of these mining regions (Photo 70). Large-scale volcanic activity with violent eruptions put billions of tons of debris into the air and spewed it over the land. The molten rock that was ejected came from magma chambers far below the surface. As these chambers were emptied explosively, the voids left behind could not hold up the mountain tops above, and major collapses occurred, forming calderas. A single caldera may be tens of miles across. The fracturing around a caldera created breccia or a complex of rock fragments and voids which filled with mineralized fluids much like the process mentioned previously. Most mineral resources in Colorado are found in these two geologic situations.

Apart from the wealth, and in several cases the environmental problems, created by mineral extraction, mining has left another legacy for Colorado. A good many of Colorado's Victorian-age towns are former mining camps built during the late 1800s and early 1900s. These towns have either become ghost towns (or at least nearly ghost towns) such as Tincup, Gilman, or Bonanza or they have become tourist destinations. The ski industry, in particular, has occupied and in most cases transformed many of these communities of the montane and subalpine. Telluride (Photo 66), Crested Butte, and other communities are now renewed, repainted, and redeveloped images of their former selves. Communities other than ski resorts of the subalpine have also evolved from mining's legacy. These include the quaint, and usually authentic, towns of Lake City, Creede, Silverton, Leadville, Victor, and others.

EPILOGUE

The high mountains of Colorado straddle the subalpine life zone and were forged in fire, their life propagated by water. Heat deep within the earth helped cause the convulsive uplifts and the volcanism that spread across parts of the state in the last 30 million years. Water and ice have eroded and sculpted the land and have given Colorado the stunning landscapes of today. Water, in varied and unique ways, also gave birth to the numerous ecosystems of the subalpine. The subalpine, as much as any place, is our ideal of Colorado.

PHOTO 64 Rock outcroppings and small topographic irregularities collect snow that can help protect trees that are growing at their upper elevation limit in the ecotone. A few trees, some showing their 'flag' form, are just able to make it in the high elevations here in the West Elk Mountains.

PHOTO 65   This thick blanket of snow in the subalpine life zone of the West Elk Mountains is typical of the subalpine areas around the state. Heavy snowfalls in the subalpine and the additional snow blown in from the alpine above give the subalpine the most total snow of any life zone in the state. The snow cover is so thick in this photograph that only a bare hint of the landforms below are visible.

PHOTO 66   Bridal Veil Falls, near Telluride, is a popular ice climbing route with the locals and climbers from far afield. The building at the top is a remnant of the hydroelectric power station developed at this obvious "water power" locale.

PHOTO 67   Engelmann spruce and subalpine fir forests, like this one near Crested Butte, dominate the ecosystems of the subalpine. These 'snow forests' can tolerate heavy snowfalls because their slender spires easily slough off the heavier snows. Most spruce-fir forests are dense tangles of trees like those seen in the upper left of the photograph. The open areas are slowly being invaded by the spruce-fir - evidence of this are the many small saplings seen in the meadows.

PHOTO 68 Although Crested Butte was at the forefront of skiing in Colorado, it has developed into one of the smaller ski areas of the state. The butte itself stands alone and is surrounded by the valleys of the East and Slate Rivers. It is the center in the state for 'extreme skiing' and often hosts the extreme games.

PHOTO 69   Vail has overtaken Aspen as the largest ski resort in Colorado, but Aspen, in this photo, has retained the class and glamour it developed during the early days of skiing after World War II. With four major ski mountains in the area, it is still a force in the ski industry of Colorado and the U.S.

PHOTO 70   The staggeringly rich mining district of Cripple Creek was created when volcanic activity formed a caldera. Mineralized fluids crept into the fractures and were deposited. Mining began here in the late nineteenth century and continues into the twenty-first. At today's gold prices billions of dollars worth of the metal were extracted from the district. Pikes Peak looms on the horizon.

PHOTO 71   The riparian ecosystem along Cochetopa Creek in the La Garita Wilderness makes up only a small percentage of the total land area. The presence of water and succulent vegetation like willows and alders in the riparian, however, provides for significant habitat for the fauna of the region. These ribbons of life are fed mostly by snowmelt from the previous winter.

PHOTO 72   The Colorado River is a life-line to much of the Southwest including northwestern Mexico. The river is nearly exhausted by human use by the time it empties into the Gulf of California. The sluggish, meandering course and the cyan color indicate the tremendous suspended load of sand, silt, and clay that the water carries into the Delta. In this photo, close to the Gulf, the river is nearly as much sediment as it is water.

PHOTO 73   Before winds can shake the snow from the bows, these trees of the subalpine lie blanketed by a recent storm. The closed nature of the spruce-fir forest is obvious in this scene near Cuchara.

PHOTO 74   These aspen near Marcellina Mountain west of Kebler Pass are just beginning their autumn color show. The West Elk Mountains are one of the premier aspen viewing locations in Colorado. Large, continuous aspen stands are impressive for their vibrant colors and their size.

PHOTO 75   Kebler Pass is one of many subalpine areas that displays a multitude of ecosystems in a mosaic of color and form. Open meadows and grasslands lose much of their summer vibrancy in the fall. But the aspens' turning makes up for the loss of colorful wildflowers and verdant, green grasses. Engelmann spruce and subalpine fir stands in the background frame this bucolic autumn scene. East and West Beckwith Mountains overlook the pass.

PHOTO 76   Engelmann spruce and subalpine fir are usually immune to the force of high winds, but on October 25, 1997 winds up to 120 miles/hour blew down large stands of trees in the Mt. Zirkel Wilderness of the Park Range near Steamboat Springs. The new, open areas may soon be invaded by pioneering aspen or revert to meadows. Eventually the spruce-fir forest will probably return.

PHOTO 77   The utter devastation of the Mt. Zirkel storm of October 1997 is seen here. The blowdown of trees reminds many of the results of the cataclysmic eruption of Mt. St. Helens in 1980. It will take centuries for this forest to fully recover from this windstorm.

PHOTO 78 This scene from Cuchara Pass displays to perfection the clonal character of aspen. Each separate aspen clone has its own color and timing in autumn. These particular clones are spreading as evidenced by the smaller trees at the peripheries of the major stands.

PHOTO 79   The aspen on Cochetopa Pass are slowly being invaded and replaced by the Engelmann spruce-subalpine fir forest. Unlike young aspens, saplings of spruce-fir can tolerate shade and will eventually out-compete the aspen for light and essential nutrients.

PHOTO 80   Obvious avalanche tracks like these in the Sawatch Range exist throughout the mountains of Colorado. Avalanches are one of our most dangerous natural hazards, especially because of the tremendous increase in use of the backcountry during the winter months. But avalanches are also a significant contributor to bio-diversity. They often clear out old forest and allow it to be replaced with shrubs and herbs - habitat for many fauna.

PHOTO 81   This U-shaped valley now occupied by Maroon Creek, near Aspen, was carved by glacial activity during the geologically recent Pleistocene epoch. It is easy to envision this trough filled by moving ice, carving the valley walls as it inched its way down-valley. The past glaciers of the subalpine in Colorado are responsible for much of the spectacular scenery of the high mountains in the state.

PHOTO 82   Mount Princeton (14,197 feet) is one of the most recognized "fourteeners" in the state. The valleys on either side of the summit were predominantly shaped by two different erosional agents. The valley to the left (south) has the distinct V-shape of valleys formed by running water. The valley to the right (north) has the common U-shape of alpine glacial erosion. The two valleys were influenced by their different exposures to solar radiation.

The soon to be Great Sand Dunes National Park. This view looks north across the dunes to the Sangre de Cristo Range. The highest peak in view is 14,294 foot Crestone Peak.

Chapter 6

A L P I N E

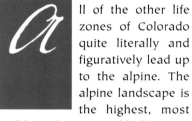

ll of the other life zones of Colorado quite literally and figuratively lead up to the alpine. The alpine landscape is the highest, most visible and recognizable life zone in the state. The often bleak and rocky summits of the high peaks stand as the quintessential Colorado - especially by those who live elsewhere and visit or dream of visiting the state. For those driving into Colorado from the east, often the most anticipated event is the first sighting of the mountains. And the mountain landscapes that are viewed first are the snowy pinnacles of the alpine zone (Photo 86). The land above the trees of the alpine may be the most photogenic and most photographed (Photo 83). It, therefore, has rightly or wrongly become the universal symbol of what Colorado is. Some altitudinal statistics will give you an idea of the dominance of high elevations on the landscape psyche of the state.

THE LAND

Colorado is the highest state, by far, in the United States. There are well over 1,100 mountains taller than 10,000 feet. Large parts of the mountain regions lie

Above

it

all

(11,500 FEET

TO

14,433 FEET)

above the 10,000 foot mark - Leadville (10,152 feet), for example, is the highest incorporated town in the United States. Over 830 peaks lie between 11,000 and 14,000 feet. There are so many that an exact count is difficult. Colorado has more than 250 mountains at 13,000 feet or higher, and many of these do not even have names! Finally, the state has 53 or 54 14ers — peaks over 14,000 feet. The discrepancy comes from how adjacent peaks are counted. The disputed mountain is Ellingwood Peak (or Point) (14,042 feet) on the Sierra Blanca (Photo 94) massif of the Sangre de Cristo Mountains. The elevation relief is just barely a 250 feet in the saddle between Blanca Peak (14,345 feet) and Ellingwood - some people feel that at least a 300 foot drop is necessary for a separation between officially designated 14,000 foot mountains.

Although the alpine life zone has one of the smallest areas of any of the life zones in the state, it has had tremendous impact on human economic development, nonetheless. The most obvious of these effects is on transportation, especially movement from east to west. Because of this, the role of the mountain pass on Colorado history has been out of all

proportion to the number of useable passes. There are a few dozen passes which have roads up and over them, and most of these roads are at best gravel and unimproved. Many are not maintained and require nerve and a very rigorous four-wheel drive vehicle to cross. Some can only be crossed on foot. There are seven passes that get as high as the alpine where the roads have been paved. The highest of these is Trail Ridge Road (12,183 feet) in Rocky Mountain National Park. One of the most scenic is Independence Pass (12,095 feet) crossing the Sawatch Range between Twin Lakes and Aspen. Cottonwood Pass (12,126 feet) is paved only on the eastern side. The other four are Loveland Pass (11,992 feet), Hoosier Pass (11,541 feet), Fremont Pass (11,318 feet), and Berthoud Pass (11,314 feet). Two other high altitude roads of Colorado that are renown worldwide are the highways up Mt. Evans (paved) (Photo 97) and Pikes Peak (gravel) (Photo 93). These routes give easy access to some of the most striking alpine landscapes one can view from a car anywhere in the United States. Both are easily accessible from major urban areas. In fact both Denver (Mt. Evans) and Colorado Springs (Pikes Peak) have been

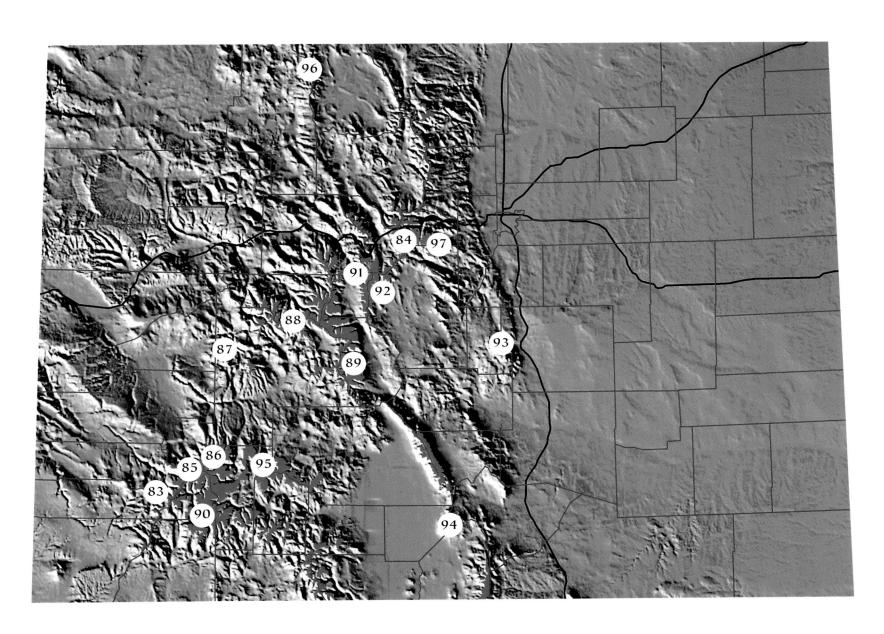

alpine

photo position

crucial to the construction and management of these highways for many years.

A common characteristic of many of the peaks over 14,000 feet and of the high passes of Colorado is that the Continental Divide passes through their highest points (Photo 84). The Continental Divide is that line that separates the flow of water going to the Pacific Ocean on the west and the Atlantic Ocean/Gulf of Mexico to the east. All seven of the paved passes listed above are traversed by the Divide. The Divide comes into the southern end of the state from New Mexico along the crest of the San Juan Mountains (Photo 90), then through the Cochetopa Hills, and along the high peaks of the Collegiate/Sawatch Range. It then bends to the east through the Tenmile Range and runs northward along the Front Range into Rocky Mountain National Park where it turns abruptly westward. It winds its way across the Rabbit Ears Range and finally turns north over the North Park Range and out of the state into Wyoming.

The Continental Divide is not only a watery divide, it also divides the state into two humanly perceived realms - the Eastern Slope and the Western Slope. Succinctly put, the eastern slope is often viewed as the urban big brother where money, population, and power dictate what happens in Colorado politics, economics, and society. The Western Slope is often seen as the holder of the true and traditional Colorado values. It supplies water and resources, but it is also relatively unpopulated and perceived as under-represented. These two views are becoming less and less accurate as the Western Slope gains economic and environmental power. The Aspens, Durangos, Vails, and Grand Junctions are seeing to that. Maybe someday the Continental Divide will just go back to being the physical barrier it was for eons. The changes in the human perceptions may sooner or later remove this mental divide between the two sides of the state.

THE GEOLOGY

The lands of Colorado have been uplifted and eroded many times in the past. This geologic activity has left a multitude of elevation zones and a variety of topographic features throughout the state. But the elevations of the alpine remain the highest for one of two reasons: first, the rock that was uplifted here is much more resistant to erosion than the surrounding rock which has long since eroded away, and/or second, the land has only recently (in geologic terms) been raised and has not yet eroded away. This is, of course, an over-simplification, but it is a useful and understandable explanation of why we still have only a few really high mountains. Most of the highest peaks in the state are because of the first reason - the rock is old, hard, crystalline, and resistant. Mt. Elbert (14,433 feet), Mt. Massive (14,421 feet), Longs Peak (14,255 feet), Pikes Peak (14,110 feet), Mt. Harvard (14,420 feet) and others are all built on cores of this hard intrusive/metamorphic rock. There are some of the high peaks that are created from sedimentary rock, (Photo 88) however, that is often less resistant to erosion. These include the region near the famous Maroon Bells and some of the peaks in the Sangre de Cristo Mountains. Whichever the case, however, these massive peaks will not be here forever. No matter how long it takes, erosion will eventually have its way. It is an irrepressible agent of nature. Water and wind, ice and gravity will someday reduce even these great mountains to mere piles of sediment being washed to the sea.

Although water is the dominant agent of erosion for all of the life zones of Colorado, glaciers have left significant landscape signatures on the high mountains of the state. Glaciers begin when the snows that fall in the winter do not all melt in the summer. Year after year, century after century, this snow slowly turns to ice and builds up to substantial thicknesses of hundreds to thousands of feet. To be a true glacier, this ice mass must move. During the Pleistocene (commonly called the Ice Ages) over the last 2 million years, innumerable glaciers slid, ground, and crept down innumerable valleys of the alpine and subalpine. The last remnants of these ice rivers did not disappear until about 10,000 years ago. A very few, small, and nearly insignificant glaciers still exist on some northern facing mountain slopes in the northern Colorado mountains. The only evidence left of the existence of most of these landscaping ice masses are the erosional and depositional glacial landforms.

These landforms are nearly everywhere in the alpine and in much of the subalpine. At the head of each glacial valley, just below the summit of the mountain, sits the cirque. This rounded and hollowed out basin is where the glacier started its run downhill. Many cirques now contain lakes (or tarns in glacial jargon) that are destinations for hikers and anglers alike (Photo 85 and 90 again). The U-shaped valleys of these glaciers are discussed in the chapter on the subalpine. Between many adjacent glacial valleys are sharp, sawtoothed ridges called aretés that are remnants of the incessant erosion that took place below. The most marked glacial landform, however, is the horn. Horns are high peaks that have cirques on multiple sides leading to various glacial valleys. The Matterhorn in Switzerland is the archetype horn. Colorado has its share of horns - some using the name horn like Wetterhorn and others just displaying the distinctive horn shape like Uncompahgre Peak (Photo 86 again), the Maroon Bells, Crestone Needle, and Mount Wilson (Photo 83 again).

THE ECOSYSTEMS

The vegetation cover of the alpine life zone is often collectively referred to as the alpine tundra. Tundra is a word that most often refers to the treeless expanses of the far north of the Arctic, but it is also applicable to high alpine environments of the middle latitudes. The vegetation in tundra environments, both Arctic and alpine, is composed of low-lying, non-tree species that have adapted to the harshness of the Arctic winter or the high elevations of the alpine. Trees need a minimum amount of heat energy during the growing season to germinate, develop, and survive. This minimum level of heat exists in neither the Arctic nor the alpine.

In this zone trees can grow if they are given a modicum of protection especially from the drying and killing winds of winter. One result is an area of 'flag' or 'banner' trees where only branches on the downwind sides of the trunks are alive. On the upwind side the branches or any new growth are killed by the severe winds in winter. The trunks provide just enough protection to keep the trees alive. Another phenomenon in this ecotone is the 'krummholz' or crooked wood zone. Here trees with the normal genetic code that determines the growth of regular spruces, firs, and some other species, will grow along the ground rather than upright. These oddly shaped trees are usually protected by snow drifts that collect in hollows or other topographic irregularities and seal the trees in a snowy cocoon for the winter. You will often see krummholz stands in bands where snow has been piled in strips that give rise to 'ribbon' forests of krummholz (Photo 96). These stands are evidence of the very tenuous and precarious nature of trees at this elevation.

The environment is so severe and unpredictable in the ecotone that most trees cannot develop viable seeds in the short growing season. Most often reproduction occurs using asexual techniques such as layering where a branch of a tree, touching the ground unmoved for a number of years, eventually develops a new root system independent of the main root system of the tree. The 'new' tree, genetically identical to the parent plant, usually grows on the downwind or lee side of the original plant because that is the most protected place. The older part of the tree may die off eventually, but the new sapling will continue to grow and develop. In this odd way the tree actually migrates downwind - an interesting and intriguing idea, to have a moving tree.

The multitude of minor and more than minor topographic variations and elevation changes in the alpine create an abundance of subtle, yet decidedly different ecosystem niches. Some areas are moist, others dry; a few protected from the incessant wind, others totally exposed; some lie under deep snow for extended periods (Photo 87), and yet others are blown snow-free by the incessant winter winds (Photo 89). Whatever the case the alpine tundra vegetation has developed a number of schemes to remain viable in these extreme environmental conditions. The one almost ubiquitous strategy for almost all alpine plants is that they grow close to the ground (Photo 95). This helps to get them out of the strongest wind gusts and close to the energy absorbing

soil surface. All but one of the alpine plant species are perennial. An annual has too much to get done in the short growing season - it must germinate, grow, flower, pollinate, and produce seed, often in the space of six to eight weeks. Perennials, on the other hand, are ready to go as soon as the temperatures and sunshine allow for photosynthesis. Stored nutrients in the root systems make the plant ready immediately in the growing season without the need to germinate seed. Some alpine plants actually produce a kind of anti-freeze or have the ability to move water outside of cell walls during freezing spells. All of the plants can reproduce sexually, in other words with seeds, but almost all of these plants reproduce mostly through non-sexual or vegetative reproduction schemes. Some put out runners, much like strawberry plants, others use underground suckers, still others can use various parts of the plant just like seeds even though seeds have not been produced. There are numerous additional strategies for reproduction, but these examples give you an idea of the unique and creative ways plants survive and thrive in this harsh environment. If and when you travel to the alpine, remember how hard these organisms work just to survive, and be careful where you step.

The aerial photographs of the alpine in this chapter are spectacular and inspiring. They show the majesty and the utter expansiveness of this, the highest life zone. But there is another way to see the intricate beauty of the alpine - on your knees looking at the tiny, delicate profusion of wildflowers during a sunny morning in mid-summer. This otherwise harsh and unforgiving environment produces flowers with the most intense colors and odors anywhere. These include the eye-catching blues of the alpine forget-me-not, the subtle pinks of the moss campion, and the reds of the rosy paintbrush. Often you will see a sea of yellow as the almost ubiquitous alpine avens floods an entire slope. Tiny king's crowns and queen's crowns, with their minute detail, make you try to look closer. Given the opportunity to travel to the alpine, take the time to really look at the plant life and wonder at how the delicate strength of these gentle flowers survive the harshest environments in all of Colorado.

HUMANS PASSING THROUGH

Examples of direct human impacts and development in the alpine are few, especially in comparison to the remainder of the mountains of Colorado. The alpine is often visited but almost never inhabited. Indigenous peoples in the high Andes Mountains of South America have adapted culturally and physiologically to life at 13 or 14,000 feet, but we have no such culture in the United States. The air is thin and the temperatures desperately cold in winter. Our visits to the very high mountains are temporary.

A few longer-term developments have occurred such as the molybdenum mine of the Climax Corporation adjacent to Fremont Pass (Photo 91). But the workers did not stay at high elevations indefinitely. At the end of each shift they commuted back down the mountain to live in the low altitudes of places like Leadville (a mere 10,000 feet or so above sea level). Obviously explorers, construction crews, and travelers use the high passes to get from one side of the mountains to the other, but few linger for long. The historical motivation to build the roads and trails over these passes usually takes one of two forms: mining or railroads (or both in many cases). Berthoud Pass, for example, was explored by Captain Edward Berthoud in 1861. He was looking for a route over the mountains for the Colorado Central Railroad between what are now Clear Creek and Grand Counties. Independence Pass was developed to link the eastern slope with the mining districts near Aspen including the now ghost town of Independence. Rollins Pass (11,671 feet), now a rugged gravel road, was the site of the Rollinsville & Middle Park Toll Road. It, too, was built for access to mining camps west of the Divide. David Moffat envisioned an easier way to get from east to west in the same location as Rollins Pass. His idea was to go under the mountain. In 1927, after Moffat's death, the 6.2 mile tunnel was finally completed. It not only had the Denver & Pacific Northwestern railroad line but also an aqueduct to carry western slope water to the thirsty cities of the Front Range.

EPILOGUE

Innumerable mining claims dot the alpine, (Photo 92) but the vast majority of productive mines were developed at elevations below the tundra. Mining did stimulate the need for travel through this high life zone, but mining infrequently occurred there. With a few exceptions such as the roads up Pikes Peak and Mt. Evans and the multitude of often eroded hiking trails to the tops of the "14ers," the alpine remains environmentally in tact. This life zone, however, is so sensitive to intrusion and disturbance, that at least three possibly major environmental threats are of concern in the future. First, as water becomes even more valuable, the cities and farmers to the east will attempt to divert more and more of it away from the natural ecosystems that depend on the reliable moisture (Photo 85 and 87 again). Second, because the alpine is viewed as the ultimate mountain landscape, more and more people will hike, camp, climb, and ATV into the life zone. This will inevitably increase environmental deterioration. Last, and maybe most threatening in the long term, because the alpine is so temperature dependent, is the rapidly increasing (by natural standards anyway) average global temperatures. These higher temperatures will surely affect the ecosystems developed over the eons in colder climes. Over the next century this may become the biggest threat to the survival of the alpine life zone as we now know it.

COLORADO'S "FOURTEENERS"

All elevations in feet

FRONT RANGE

Gray's Peak	14,270
Torrey's Peak	14,267
Mt. Evans	14,264
Long's Peak	14,255
Pike's Peak	14,110
Mt. Bierstadt	14,060

MOSQUITO RANGE

Mt Lincoln	14,286
Quandry Peak	14,265
Mt. Boss	14,172
Mt. Democrat	14,148
Mt. Sherman	14,036

SAWATCH RANGE

Mt. Elbert	14,433
Mt. Massive	14,421
Mt. Harvard	14,420
La Plata Peak	14,336
Mt. Antero	14,269
Mt. Shavano	14,229
Mt. Belford	14,197
Mt. Princeton	14,197
Mt. Yale	14,196
Tabeguache Mountain	14,155
Mt. Oxford	14,153
Mt. Columbia	14,073
Missouri Mountain	14,067
Mt. Of the Holy Cross	14,005
Huron Peak	14,003

SANGRE DE CRISTO MOUNTAINS

Blanca Peak	14,345
Crestone Peak	14,294
Crestone Needle	14,197
Kit Carson Peak	14,165
Humboldt Peak	14,064
Culebra Peak	14,047
Ellingwood Peak	14,042
Mt. Lindsey	14,042
Little Bear Peak	14,037

ELK MOUNTAINS

Castle Peak	14,265
South Maroon Peak	14,156
Capitol Peak	14,130
Snowmass Mountain	14,092
Pyramid Peak	14,018
North Maroon Peak	14,014

SAN JUAN MOUNTAINS

Uncompahgre Peak	14,309
Mt. Wilson	14,246
El Dienete Peak	14,159
Mt. Sneffels	14,150
Mt. Eolus	14,083
Windom Peak	14,082
Sunlight Peak	14,059
Handies Peak	14,048
Redcloud Peak	14,034
Wilson Peak	14,017
Wetterhorn Peak	14,015
San Luis Peak	14,014
Sunshine Peak	14,001

PHOTO 83   Lizard Head, which looms over Lizard Head Pass in the western San Juans, is a very distinctive rock formation and is carved from the remains of Tertiary volcanic activity that occurred throughout the San Juan Mountains. Mt. Wilson (14,246 feet) rises above Lizard Head to the northwest. The geologically recent mountain building in the San Juans gives many of its peaks an austere and stark look.

PHOTO 84 Grays Peak, on the Continental Divide, (14,270 feet) is another of the Front Range "fourteeners" which include Longs Peak, Torreys Peak, Mt. Evans, and Pikes Peak. All of these mountains have cores consisting of ancient intrusive and metamorphic rock that was formed at great depth and during a time more than a billion years ago. The rocks of the mountains we see now were once far below the surface of the earth and were uplifted thousands of feet to their present heights.

PHOTO 85   Lake Hope in the San Juan Mountains is one of the innumerable mountain lakes of the alpine. Hope, like so many of these lakes, was created by the erosion caused by thick valley glaciers that ran down the mountain valleys as recently as 10,000 years ago. It sits in the glacial cirque that was at the head of the large alpine glacier that once filled the valley below.

PHOTO 86 Uncompahgre Peak is one of the most recognizable mountains in the San Juan Range. Its distinctive profile can be seen for tens of miles in almost all directions. At an elevation of 14,309 feet, it is the highest mountain in the San Juans. The San Juans are one of the youngest and most rugged ranges in all of Colorado. Uncompahgre Peak is indicative of this with its steep and rocky slopes.

PHOTO 87 The West Elk Mountains usually have a very heavy snowfall in the alpine regions of the range. Not only does the snow provide for great skiing and other winter sports, it produces a crucial part of the water that flows into the Gunnison River drainage system and on to the Colorado River.

PHOTO 88   The sedimentary rock layers at the crest of Castle Peak (14,265 feet) are unusual for most of the high mountains of Colorado. Sedimentary rocks generally erode much faster than the usual hard, crystalline rocks of the high peaks. Some of the few other sedimentary rock peaks in the state are the near neighbors of Castle, South Maroon Peak (14,156 feet), and North Maroon Peak (14,014 feet) in the Elk Mountain Range near Aspen.

PHOTO 89 The Sawatch Mountain Range has the highest peaks in the state - Mt. Elbert (14,433 feet), Mt. Massive (14,421 feet), and Mt. Harvard (14,420 feet). The Continental Divide runs north/south all along the crest of this impressive mountain wall. The county motto for Chaffee County which lies along the eastern flank of the Sawatch Range is, "Now This Is Colorado" - an apt slogan. This photo shows strong winds scouring snow from the higher peaks.

PHOTO 90 This photo is in the rugged and spectacular Weminuche Wilderness Area of the San Juan Mountains. The Continental Divide runs along the crests of the peaks in this scene. The Weminuche has some of the best-preserved alpine landscapes in the entire state and is one of the most remote and wild Wilderness Areas in Colorado.

PHOTO 91 The Climax Molybdinum Mine at the crest of Fremont Pass just south of Leadville is one of the largest mining operations ever in Colorado. The closing of the mine has had great economic impacts on the region and leaves many environmental questions about such large-scale mining unanswered.

PHOTO 92   These lonely looking mine remnants sit high above the old mining community of Alma - just on the south side of Hoosier Pass. The town of Alma still exists as one of the most authentic remaining mining towns in the state, although it is slowly becoming a bedroom community for the far more glitzy town of Breckenridge just over Hoosier Pass.

PHOTO 93   Pikes Peak (14,110 feet) stands at the very southern end of the long and relatively narrow Front Range of Colorado. It has a gravel road to the very peak that is used by thousands of visitors each year. This 'highway' is open for most of the year, but driving it in the winter can be a real adventure. The famous slogan, "Pikes Peak or Bust," actually referred to the gold rush to the area just west of present day Denver 70 miles to the north. This view looks northwest across South Park.

PHOTO 94   The Blanca Peak (14,345 feet) massif covers a very large area of land in the alpine in the Sangre de Cristo Mountains. Its broad shoulders have several other peaks that rise to significant heights such as Ellingwood Peak (14,042 feet) just to Blanca's northwest (right) and Mt. Lindsey (also at 14,042 feet) to the east (out of view). Blanca is one of the Navajos' four sacred mountains - the home of White Shell Woman, an important Navajo deity. The eastern boundary of the soon to be Great Sand Dunes National Park is at the extreme lower right. This photo looks south, and the Blanca summit is the far peak in the photo center.

PHOTO 95   The La Garita Wilderness Area of the eastern San Juan Mountains is well known for its extensive alpine meadows and high, rolling alpine landscapes. The area is also known for its profusion of wild flowers in the mid- to late-summer months. The vegetation in these alpine regions is always low in stature and only visible at close range. The La Garita is a place to really get away from it all because it is far from roads and not easily accessible.

PHOTO 96   The obvious ribbon forests on these high slopes in the Mount Zirkel Wilderness Area result from the rippled snow drift patterns of winter. Above the ribbon forest, the low-lying dark green vegetation is typical krummholz where the normally upright and stately spruces grow along the ground to avoid the winter's killing winds.

PHOTO 97   Mt. Evans (14,264 feet) provides the high mountain backdrop for the city of Denver. The highest paved road in the United States seen here winding up the mountain, takes you within a few tens of feet of the actual summit. The road going up Mt. Evans gives people very easy access to spectacular alpine landscapes. Along the highway are two places where travelers can leave their cars and easily experience the alpine firsthand - the Mt. Goliath Natural Area and Summit Lake.

Day breaks over Humboldt and Crestone Peaks, Sangre de Cristo Range, Custer County.

What we call the upper Sonoran life zone in Colorado is essentially the northeastern end of the Colorado Plateau - that 130,000 square mile land of layered rocks, flat-topped mesas, and deeply incised canyons famous in the Southwest. This western edge of Colorado is far different both in human legacies and natural landscapes than the other 80 percent of the state. This is a seemingly mystical land that echoes of civilizations long past and thoroughly distinctive landscapes. It is a land that is high above sea level (most of it over a mile) with rapid changes in elevation, yet from many vantage points it looks flat and unremarkable. It takes some getting to know for most people before they realize the splendor and charm of this enchanted land. It is an enigmatic landscape that fascinates and lures those who learn the most about it.

THE LAND

The Colorado Plateau in general and the upper Sonoran lands of Colorado in particular are marked by distinctive geologic structural history. The

Dry Land -

Flat Rock

(6,000 FEET

TO

7,500 FEET

in the West)

mountains to the east were uplifted several times over past eons in what geologists call orogenic events. These are very intense, yet relatively localized, uplifts that produced considerable folding, fracturing, and faulting of the rock. Because of this the mountain geology is often very complex. The rocks of the plateaus, on the other hand, were lifted en masse, or nearly so. This kind of uplift regime is called an epirogenic even (much more widespread) and it produces many fewer folds and faults. An analogy for the plateaus would be lifting up a multi-layered cake that is sitting in your hands (Photo 101). The cake generally goes up with only minor bending or breaking depending upon how steady your hands are. Of course this is a simplistic description since there is such a vast area of uplift for the Colorado Plateau, but the result is that most of the rock layers or strata are in tact as they are uplifted.

The rocks themselves that make up the plateaus are almost totally sedimentary. There are some old crystalline rocks deep within some of the canyons, but these are overlain by hundreds, if not thousands, of feet of sedimentary rock (Photo 106) and a few volcanic cap rocks or terranes. These sedimentary

rocks are the remains of older rock that was once uplifted, eroded, and deposited again. The type of rock produced depended on the original parent rock type, the environment within which the newer rock was laid down, and time. Some of these rocks (e.g. Entrada sandstone) resemble the older sand dunes of a once drier era. Some (e.g. Morrison formation) contain the fossils of dinosaurs which roamed wet lowlands and marshes. Some provided host rocks for the region's vast oil shale reserves (Photo 107). Some (e.g. Dakota sandstone) are lithified sands of beaches which occurred along the littorals of ancient shallow seas. And still others (e.g. Mancos shale) (Photo 102) are the fine detritus that settled out into the muds in the water of the ancient seas. A few of these rocks are very resistant to erosion, others erode easily. Often the rocks resistant to erosion will cap or protect weaker rock below. This idea of cap rock and different (or differential) erosion is what makes the plateau regions so interesting and unique.

Just as with the mountains, as the sedimentary rocks of the plateaus were raised up, the

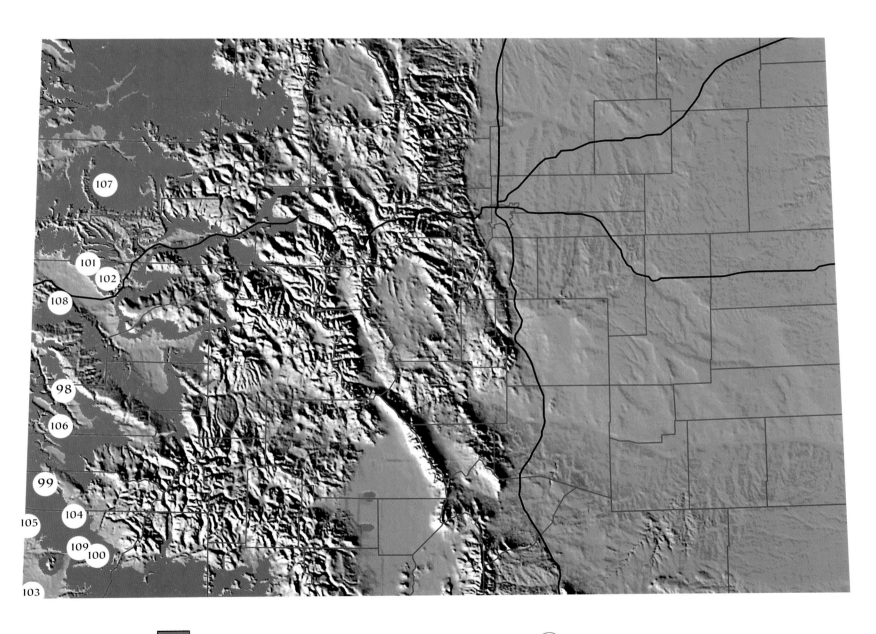

upper sonoran   ◯ photo position

potential energy of running water increased the cutting down by erosion. As the land lifts up rapidly, erosion cuts down rapidly. Only where there is a localized weakness in the generally hard cap rock, however, will the running water cut down with any speed into the softer rock below. The almost endless canyons of the plateau region are the result of this phenomenon. It is a geologic irony that in a dry, often arid, place like western Colorado, running water is the main agent for the landforms that exist. But because the low precipitation rates do not produce very extensive vegetation cover to protect the ground, when rain does come the water can run fast and erode quickly. One of the most hazardous places to be during a desert thunderstorm is in one of the "dry" arroyos that criss-cross the land. In breathtaking (maybe life-taking) speed, the arroyos can fill with debris-laden water rushing down seemingly peaceful canyons and washes. Many a campsite or hiker has been washed away and subsequently buried beneath the sediment-heavy water.

But it is the canyons, of course, that make the plateau country the place that it is. Ask anyone what the most spectacular landscapes of the Southwest are, and the Grand Canyon or Canyonlands National Park or Bryce Canyon or Zion National Park will surely be amongst the answers. Western Colorado has its share of beautiful canyon country too. Colorado National Monument (Photo 108), for example, is a place where canyons, mesas, and erosional remnants (monuments!) are found in abundance. The hard Kayenta formation caps the thick Wingate sandstone. Where the Kayenta is breached, the Wingate erodes to form vertical walls hundreds of feet into the canyon below. Canyons proliferate as in Paradox Valley (Photo 106 again), in the Uncompahgre Plateau, and in the very southwestern areas near Mesa Verde National Park and Ute Mountain Tribal Park (Photo 100). Dinosaur National Monument in the northwest has canyons aplenty and sports one of the world's largest collections of dinosaur fossils locked in the ancient muds of the Morrison formation deep in the canyons of the Yampa and Green Rivers. The upper Sonoran life zone

of Colorado is part of the Colorado Plateau, and it is the canyons of this country that make the landscapes remarkable.

THE ECOSYSTEMS

The list of environmental factors that define the upper Sonoran of Colorado coincide almost perfectly with the pattern of the piñon/juniper woodland in the western part of the state - annual precipitation rates of twelve to eighteen inches; long frost-free periods; high evaporation rates; strong and persistent winds; intense sunshine for much of the year; and very warm summers. In fact if you were to map the distribution of piñon/juniper woodland in western Colorado, you would be well on your way to accurately mapping the upper Sonoran life zone.

The piñon pine and Utah juniper of western Colorado are trees with much in common. They are both relatively short evergreen coniferous trees with wide profiles. Their foliage has a waxy substance that helps prevent excessive evaporation of precious moisture. And they almost always grow together in large stands. The Utah junipers are more dominant at lower and drier elevations and the piñons are more vigorous at the higher and slightly wetter altitudes. Often the junipers will act as nursery trees for the piñons - because the junipers are more robust in drier conditions, they will invade and grow first. The shade they offer moderates the micro-climate enough for young piñons to get established in the junipers' shadows. Both the piñon pine and the Utah juniper have chemical defenses to help in their survival. These chemicals discourage foraging by herbivores because of the pungent taste produced, and the chemicals also ward off the growth of other plants under or near the trees. This helps the trees to garner as much of the invaluable moisture as possible. These chemical defenses are obvious to we humans too. The junipers, for example, emit a pungent odor that we recognize as the smell of gin. Gin gets its distinctive aroma from these juniper berries. Piñon pines also possess aromatic chemicals. In this case, however, burning piñons give off the recognizable sweet smoke so familiar in places like Taos and Santa Fe, New Mexico. This is definitely a ubiquitous symbol for the upper Sonoran of

Colorado and the entire Southwest region of the United States.

A second ecosystem encountered in the upper Sonoran is the shrubland ecosystem including the sagebrush expanses of the semi-arid areas. Large tracts of sage can stretch for miles, especially northwest of Dolores on what is called the Great Sage Plain. Distant slopes covered in sage can have a purplish tint - thus the name "land of the purple sage." There are a number of sage species in Colorado, but most of the upper Sonoran sage is the big sage, a four to six foot tall, large shrub. The upper Sonoran may be the most aromatic region of Colorado because the sage adds its own very pleasant and distinctive odors to the landscape. The aroma and taste are so unique that sage is used in many local foods.

Competition in the upper Sonoran for water and soil nutrients is so intense that, as mentioned above, many plants such as the piñon/juniper produce chemical deterrents to encroachment by other plants. This is also the case for the big sage and many of the other shrubs of the region. The effects of this chemical warfare are termed allelochemic and can be caused by a wide variety of toxins. Some of these are only moderately toxic to other plants; some are extremely poisonous including some very harsh alkaloids and organic cyanide.

In addition to the big sage, several other shrub species grow in this life zone and are usually found in some of the driest conditions. These plants are drought resistant and have devised many adaptations to help them survive, if not thrive, in this land of little water. Some of these adaptations include resistance to salt saturated soils and succulent foliage that helps prevent excessive evaporation and transpiration. Examples of these hardy plants are greasewood, four-wing saltbush, shadscale, and winterfat.

The most interesting ecosystem of the upper Sonoran, however, may be the riparian zone. In contrast to the often harsh and formidable ecosystems of the piñon/juniper and the shrublands, the riparian ecosystems can be found in the deep canyons. The riparian here is much like the riparian of the other life zones - it is a place of fecund life and prolific variety.

But the contrast between the stark arid to semi-arid environments at the mesa tops or the sage-covered plains of the upper Sonoran and the canyon-bottom riparian here is so dramatic that these green and lush ribbons of life are almost shocking. The variety of species is large and includes plants such as willows, bog birch, cottonwoods, cinquefoil, aspen, poison ivy, sedges, and lush grasses. Even species like Douglas fir and blue spruce can be found with regularity. An invasive species of flora that is becoming a serious threat to the riparian diversity is the tamarisk. The tamarisk, or salt cedar, is an exotic shrub with few natural controls in the southwestern United States. It has been steadily out-competing species like the variety of willows and the cottonwoods for dominance. It is a voracious user of precious water and threatens the integrity of much of the riparian in the whole region.

Because of the profusion of vegetation types, the riparian is also the main habitat area for many of the region's fauna. Mountain lion, black bear, mule deer, an abundance of reptiles and amphibians (including rattlesnakes, toads, frogs, and lizards), and a multitude of bird species all inhabit or use the riparian. At times it seems like it is bursting with life in stark contrast to the more marginal ecosystems of the more arid areas.

One common characteristic of all of the ecosystems of the upper Sonoran is that small changes in elevation and/or aspect can create significant changes in environment. Generally, the higher the elevation, the wetter and cooler the land gets relative to its surroundings. It is easy to see these dramatic changes in just a few feet of rise if you look at the highest mesas and hillslopes - vegetation can change abruptly with only minor changes in altitude. Add to this the impact of aspect that creates shaded environments, and you have a region of tremendous variety and interest.

The Human Landscapes

During the summer of 1776, when the fledgling Continental Congress proclaimed independence for the thirteen colonies lying along the eastern coast of North America, a small and intrepid group of explorers were searching for a route from New Mexico to California. Padres Francisco Atanasia Dominguez and Silvestre Vélez de Escalante left Santa Fe and traveled through much of southwestern Colorado toward the north and west into Utah in a vain search for easy passage to California. The Spanish had been in North America for well over 200 years before the Dominguez and Escalante expedition and had established European influence on the continent even before Jamestown and Plymouth.

Yet, as distant in the past as the Spanish colonization in North America seems, Dominguez and Escalante discovered ruins of a civilization some 1,500 years older than the earliest Conquistadors. This culture is often named the Anasazi, but is more correctly called the Ancestral Puebloans. Two of the ruins found by the Spanish are named the Dominguez and the Escalante (Photo 104) sites and are located on the grounds of the Anasazi Heritage Center near Dolores - Dolores being named after the river originally christened *El Rio de Nuestra Señora de los Dolores* by the Spanish. But even these ancestral Puebloans were newcomers to the region. There is substantial evidence that people have been in this part of the state for well over 10,000 years. These Paleo-Indians, as archaeologists call them, have left only a few material pieces of evidence. These include uniquely made projectile points and ancient butchering and occupation sites.

Because the old Puebloans left so much physical evidence of their occupation, their existence has been the most intensely studied and creates the most popular interest. From the early Basketmaker period of the Anasazi (1 A.D. to about 750 A.D.), we find pottery, relatively crude houses and storage facilities, and the rudimentary beginnings of organized agriculture. As the Anasazi advanced they built more elaborate pit houses, ceremonial kivas, and irrigation works (Photo 105). They also improved farming to the point where grown crops were much more important to their diet than food obtained through hunting or gathering. This later Pueblo period peaked around 1150 to 1200 A.D. when they began building the phenomenal cliff dwellings we marvel at today in places such as Mesa Verde National Park. The southwestern corner of Colorado was only the far northern outpost of a civilization centered near Chaco Canyon, New Mexico. Elaborate trading routes, cultural and religious exchanges, and common life styles connected the Anasazi from as far away as the Grand Canyon in the southwest to central Utah in the northwest. Hundreds of years of cultural development produced this impressive civilization. Then suddenly around 1300, they disappeared from the canyons and abandoned their irrigated fields. Rampant speculation about their departure still dominates archaeological studies - why did they leave and where did they go? Most likely it was a combination of factors including drought and possible environmental collapse, changes in religious customs which promoted connections with the Pueblo cultures along the Rio Grande valley, and/or conflicts with more aggressive cultures invading their territory. Whatever the reason(s) for their departure, their lives in the Four Corners region left behind a treasure of ruins scattered over thousands of square miles of canyon country.

Official influence of Spain over Mexico ended in 1821 when Mexico gained its independence. That independence also ended the Spanish policy of denying trade between Mexico and the lands to the north, including this area of western Colorado. Mexican influence and migration to southern and western Colorado was slow but steady over the next several decades. But any doubt of the contribution to the area by both Spain and Mexico is soon dispelled as you look at the names throughout the region - Cortez, Dolores, Purgatoire, Durango, Hermosa, La Plata, San Juan, Montezuma, San Miguel, and hundreds of others.

Much of the exploration of the region by the Spanish and Mexicans was to search for gold. This is the same reason that Anglo-Americans moved into the area (mostly to the mineral rich mountains) and forcibly or legally (many would say illegally) removed the Utes from their homelands. The Utes had been here for several hundred years. But in a rapid succession of broken promises and forced treaties, the Utes were finally pushed into Utah or onto a thin strip of land along the southern border of Colorado. The "Meeker Massacre" of 1879 was the final big event in Ute/Anglo warfare after which the nomadic Utes were totally subjugated.

Not all Anglos, however, came for mineral riches; many came to begin farms and ranches. The southwestern end of the Uncompahgre Plateau was an especially desirable place for land. It was relatively fertile, had somewhat higher precipitation rates than many places in the life zone, and had potential irrigation water nearby. The small community of Naturita was founded to take advantage of the irrigation possibilities of Naturita Creek and the San Miguel River. The settlement of Nucla was begun as a "communal" farming enterprise by the Colorado Cooperative Company in 1896. Other towns such as Norwood on the plateau and Dove Creek and Pleasant View to the southwest are still farming centers where beans, alfalfa, fruit, and corn are grown and processed. Cortez is not only considered the "Center of United States Archaeology" because of the Anasazi influence, it is also the center for pinto bean production in Colorado (Photo 99). Along with tourism, agriculture was, and still is, a main segment for the economy of the entire region. Mining is less influential here than in the nearby San Juan Mountains, but it has some strong local impacts nonetheless.

Gold, silver, and other metals found in the mountains were the original attraction to the Anglos. But other minerals have been central to the economy of the upper Sonoran region over the last hundred years. This is especially true near the former town of Uravan. In fact the name Uravan is derived from two elements found in the locally abundant mineral carnotite - uranium and vanadium. A third valuable element, radium, is also found in carnotite. Radium was the first of this triad to be used scientifically and commercially. Some of the radium from the area was used by Marie Curie in her Nobel winning experiments in France. Vanadium was the next to become commercially viable. It seems that vanadium has the ability to make steel very hard. This property was discovered in the 1930s, and the advent of World War II substantially increased the value of this element. Soon, however, uranium became the most critical element of the three. Sixty percent of the uranium for the Manhattan Project came from this area. And uranium was coveted after the war, not only for nuclear weapons, but for the rapidly growing nuclear power industry. As demand for nuclear power has waned, so have the economic prospects of Uravan and the other uranium mining communities. Union Carbide, the owner of Uravan, has closed the mine and literally removed the town. All that remains are the skeletal vestiges of mining past and the massive environmental cleanup effort of the site (Photo 98).

Epilogue

The table-top mesas and the deeply incised canyons of the upper Sonoran life zone of Colorado remind us much more of the landscapes of the Southwest than those of the high mountains of the state (Photo 103). In some ways this land is an inscrutable mosaic of rock and sky, desert and mountain, canyon and plain. (Photo 109) At times it may seem almost mystical, especially when considering the ancient past of the first human cultures that developed, matured, and assuredly vanished with time. The wondrous, built environment of the Anasazi reminds us, much like the missing town of Uravan, that the world progresses with or without us or our material things. Inevitably, the land and cultures here are so old and so unique that we view them differently than all the other places in this, the Centennial State.

This is the fitting last chapter in this book. Hopefully, it is a tempting chapter - tempting enough so that you will want to see for yourself the natural and human landscapes throughout the state. We wish you good travel, sudden insights, and enjoyment - most of all enjoyment in the great place we call Colorado.

PHOTO 98   Uravan (a name formed by combining uranium and vanadium) was one of the country's most important uranium mines during and after World War II. It has since been closed, and the only work now is cleaning up this Super Fund Site.

PHOTO 99 Although the climate in the upper Sonoran is semi-arid to arid, it is still an area of considerable agricultural activity. One of the staples of this farming industry are the pinto beans - fields of pinto beans are shown in this photo near Dove Creek.

PHOTO 100   Sleeping Ute Mountain in the distance is the landscape symbol for the Ute Mountain Indian Reservation in far southwestern Colorado. The foreground of this photo is Mesa Verde National Park, site of the most spectacular ancient dwellings of the ancestral Puebloans. The green vegetated mesa tops have given the Mesa Verde (green) its name.

PHOTO 101   The Book Cliffs are a long, undulating sedimentary formation that lies at the very northern end of the Colorado Plateau in Colorado and Utah. The cliffs can be seen for dozens of miles along the northern horizon as you follow the Colorado River westward from Grand Junction.

PHOTO 102 The eerie erosional landscapes created from the ubiquitous Mancos shale of the upper Sonoran are seen in this photo. This soft rock can be recognized throughout the region by its subdued landforms and dark, grayish color.

PHOTO 103 This solitary ranchstead shows the dry character of much of southwestern Colorado. This collection of ranch structures is part of a property owned by a Navajo family in the four-corners area of Colorado.

PHOTO 104 These ruins of ancestral Puebloans were discovered by the Dominguez/Escalante expedition of 1776. This particular site was named after Silvestre Vélez de Escalante and is only a short walk from the Anasazi Heritage Center near Dolores.

PHOTO 105 Mesa Verde has a high concentration of ancestral Puebloan ruins. Hovenweep National Monument has a truly extensive array of ruins spread over hundreds of square miles in Colorado and Utah. One of the signature architectural designs for many structures in Hovenweep are these tall, thin towers that dot the landscape.

PHOTO 106 Paradox Valley shown in this photo is both unique and very typical of the innumerable water-cut canyons of the upper Sonoran life zone. The bedded sandstones of the plateau are easily recognized after being exposed by the relentless erosion. But in this case the current stream in the valley cuts across the valley, not along it - hence the name Paradox. The La Sal Mountains of Utah are on the far horizon.

PHOTO 107 The far northwestern corner of Colorado contains one of the world's largest reserves of potential oil (called kerogen) held fast in the rock popularly called "oil shale." This retort is one of two built to test the feasibility of extracting usable oil from the Green River formation well below the surface. The oil shale program has been abandoned, at least for the foreseeable future.

PHOTO 108   The great bend of the monoclinal fold that was created when the Colorado Plateau, including the Colorado National Monument area seen here, was uplifted at the very northern edge of the plateau. The Colorado National Monument has some of the most spectacular cliffs in the West that were created when water cut down through the upper layers of rock and exposed the monolithic Wingate sandstone below.

PHOTO 109   This view of Mesa Verde National Park is very different from the one in Photo 100. Fires during the summer of 2000 burned large parts of the Park. It will take many years for the vegetation to recover. Notice the orange stripe at the bottom center of the photo that came from the slurry dropped from aircraft during the fire - it looks like it stopped fire from over-topping the ridge. Smoke from the smoldering fire still hangs in the air.

BIBLIOGRAPHY

Barcott, B., 1997. *The Measure of a Mountain: Beauty and Terror on Mount Rainier*, New York: Ballantine Books.

Benedict, A. D., 1991. *The Southern Rockies: A Sierra Club Naturalist's Guide*, San Francisco: Sierra Club Books.

Carter, J. L., 1988. *Trees and Shrubs of Colorado*, Boulder, CO: Johnson Books.

Eberhart, P., 1969. *Guide to the Colorado Ghost Towns and Mining Camps*, Chicago, IL: Swallow Press.

Eichler, G.R., 1977. *Colorado Place Names*, Boulder, CO: Johnson Books.

Evans, H. E. and M. A. Evans, 1991. *Cache la Poudre: The Natural History of a Rocky Mountain River*, Niwot, CO: University Press of Colorado.

Fuller, M., 1989. *Mountains: A Natural History and Hiking Guide*, New York: John Wiley & Sons, Inc.

Harper, K. T., L. L. St. Clair, K. H. Thorne, and W. M. Hess, eds., 1994. *Natural History of the Colorado Plateau and Great Basin*, Niwot, CO: University Press of Colorado.

Huber, T. P., 1997. *Colorado Byways: A Guide Through Scenic and Historic Landscapes*, Niwot, CO: University Press of Colorado.

Huber, T. P., 1993. *Colorado: The Place of Nature, the Nature of Place*, Niwot, CO: University Press of Colorado.

Huber, T. P. and R. P. Larkin, 1996. *The San Luis Valley of Colorado: A Geographical Sketch*, Colorado Springs: The Hulbert Center for Southwestern Studies.

Metzger, S., 1992 (or later). *Colorado Handbook*, Chico, CA: Moon Publications Inc.

Meyers, C., 1987. *Colorado Ski Country*, Helena, MT: Falcon Press.

Quammen, D., 1996. *The Song of the Dodo*, New York, NY: Touchstone.

Rennicke, J., 1985. *The Rivers of Colorado*, Helena, MT: Falcon Press.

Stegner, W.E. 1954. *Beyond the Hundredth Meridan*, Boston: Houghton Mifflin.

Trefil, J., 1986. *Meditations at 10,000 Feet: A Scientist in the Mountains*, New York: Charles Scribner's Sons.

Varney, P. and J. Drew, 1999. *Ghost Towns of Colorado*, Stillwater, MN: Voyageur Press.

Veblen, T. T. and D. C. Lorenz, 1991. *The Colorado Front Range: A Century of Ecological Change*, Salt Lake City: University of Utah Press.

Wolf, T., 1995. *Colorado's Sangre de Cristo Mountains*, Niwot, CO: University Press of Colorado.

ACKNOWLEDGMENTS

We would like to thank John Harner and Dana Mangold for their help in collecting and organizing the data we used for the chapter maps. We especially want to thank Philippe Waterinckx for his aid in developing the maps into usable and attractive parts of the book. Finally, without the enthusiasm of Roberta Ringstrom (our colleague and student), we would never have gotten together to do this book.

TAKING THE PICTURES

The photography for this book was done using the following equipment and methods:

CAMERAS: Leica 35 mm; R6 & M6. These Leica cameras are very rugged with no automatic features (exposure, focus, or winding), thus each photo is a studied and individual creation of the photographer, not the camera.

LENSES: A total eleven fixed focus Leitz lenses (seven R & four M) ranging from 28 mm to 180 mm focal lengths, and f 1.4 to f 2.8 maximum apeture, were used.

FILM: The only film used was Fuji RVP (Velvia), ASA 50. This is a very fine grained, color saturated film which is superbly suited for aerial photography of the character done for this book.

AIRCRAFT: The airplane used was a Christen (now Aviat) A-1 Husky; a small single-engine, 180 hp, high wing, bush-type aircraft. The Husky has centerline seating with a large side-opening which makes it ideal for single-operator aerial photography.

All of the photography was done by the pilot. Most of the shots were taken at an altitude of about 1500 feet above the ground, with the lowest at 500 feet, and the highest probably 3000 feet. Depending on the light intensity, shutter speeds of 1/1000 to 1/125 second were used. Most photos were taken at full, or close to full, lens opening. The aircraft was slowed to an airspeed of about seventy mph for most work. More than two thousand photographs and some one hundred hours of flying contributed to the final product. All the photos in the book were taken from the air.

Christen Husky

Navajo Lake lies nestled in the bosom of this "u" shaped glacial valley. This view looks east to El Diente Peak, and beyond to Mt. Wilson in Dolores County.

INDEX

INDEX

INDEX

Lenticular clouds, evidence of high winds aloft, cap the Spanish Peak at sunset, Huerfano Co...